SEARCHING
for my
Heart

SEARCHING

for my

Heart

essays about love

Dawn Downey

PATHLESS LAND PRESS
KANSAS CITY MO

Published 2018 by Pathless Land Press
Printed in the United States of America

ISBN 978-0-9963240-5-2

Cover design by Teresa Mandala
www.bella-designs.biz

Book Design by Maureen Cutajar
www.gopublished.com

Author photo by Stephen Locke
www.stephenlocke.com

For Ben,
my vitamin B

CONTENTS

PART I
Relations

A TRAVELER'S TALE

I

Des Moines. August.

I squatted on the stairs after a round of hopscotch, while a mosquito buzzed around me. After it found the thin skin on the inside of my arm, I smacked it, but another took its place. A third landed on my ankle. A final smack, and I returned to picking at a scab—an injury caused by jumping from the top step the day before, believing I could fly. I'd crashed onto the bricks, more shocked by the fact of gravity than hurt by the impact. The wound stung but didn't bleed, and the fall left a gouge in my elbow, like I'd scooped out a spoonful of flesh. Afterward I'd searched on hands and knees, trying to find the missing piece of me.

Heat waves shimmered over our brick sidewalk, which divided the front yard in half from stoop to curb—the bricks in a chevron pattern with dandelions growing in the cracks. *Step on a crack; break your mother's back.* Beside the porch, marigolds soaked up the sun that baked the earth beneath them. Yellow and orange blooms stood out like colored sprinkles accidentally spilled in the parched brown grass. In a corner of the yard, where the grass sloped down to meet the street, a buckeye tree spread a ring of shade.

My cousins and siblings—along with a few neighborhood kids—prowled the streets in a Lord-of-the-Flies tribe that inflicted damage on body and spirit, according to shifting alliances. I hung around the periphery. *Sticks and stones will break my bones, but words will never hurt me.* A lie. Words caved me in and sent me running back to the house.

"What's wrong with her?"

"Who cares?"

Firefly lights circled my finger like a diamond ring, as if I had been chosen—maybe by the boy who sat two desks over from me at school. As if I knew how to be chosen. That was me on the sidelines when the tribe played baseball. "Don't pick her. She strikes out." Me, hiding in the bathroom when they rode bikes. And me, sneaking out the back door when the others gathered in the house to play Cootie. Cootie gave me nightmares.

Days ended in hide-and-seek—one last ritual to endure until the streetlights announced suppertime. *It* leaned into the buckeye tree and counted to ten. I raced to our back yard, past the clothesline tented with sheets, past a patch of wild rhubarb. Seconds before "Ready or not, here I come," I kneeled behind the garage. Clods of hard clay poked dents in my palms, and the sticky twilight left no place for forehead sweat to go except into my eyes. A bumpy rash between my fingers itched like crazy, but scratching only intensified the itch. I squished a mosquito on my leg, and the burst body left behind a slime of blood, legs, and wings that I wiped into the dirt.

Garage doors crashed open. Footsteps crunched the gravel drive, predator in pursuit of prey. Huffing. A body thudded against a tree trunk.

"Safe."

"Nuh-uh. Gotcha."

"You wish."

A rock thwacked against flesh, then hit pavement.

"Ow. Jerk."

After the last person made it home safe, I sat back on the ground. A push mower clacked in a yard across the alley, and the smell of new-mown grass floated me away from heat blisters and Cootie and *what's wrong with her*. Away to Anywhere, Not Iowa, U.S.A.

The fantasy would come true. I would travel from Iowa to Anywhere and back again. But I was a hummingbird, furiously beating my wings to stay in one place, hovering over the sweetness, unable to make a home of any single bloom.

II

Santa Barbara. July.

The tide sucked sand from under my feet and threw me off balance. Kelp snaked around my ankles. The receding surf blanketed my toes with foam and left them icy, even as the sun warmed my shoulders. Gulls screamed at a collie twisting in mid-leap to catch a Frisbee. I backed away from the water and strolled uphill to join my best friend, Angie Mendoza, waving to me from a picnic table.

We were spending the night on East Beach with her cousins. We had a job to do: stake a claim on a spot for the next day's Fourth of July picnic. Mothers and *abuelas* would arrive early in the morning to cook chorizo, but the night belonged to us teenagers. We danced, gossiped, and smoked pot. I flirted with Angie's doe-eyed, long-lashed third cousin from Tijuana, overlooking the fact he did not flirt back. As we wandered along the beach to see who else was camping, "Stoned Soul Picnic" blasted from a car stereo and blended into Jose Feliciano singing "Light My Fire" a few cars down. The tunes were as familiar as Angie's patchouli, a fragrance too delicate to obscure my discomfort at the all-Spanish conversation poking through the night music. Despite straight-A diligence in high school Spanish and weekend immersions into the Mendoza household, I was stuck at *almost* fluent—Angie's black friend, almost *mija*.

When we finally crawled into our sleeping bags, stars polka-dotted an inky sky. Phosphorescent waves rolled in. Plankton, caught up inside the foam, dipped and twirled incandescence along the beach. Beyond the froth, the deep. An abyss that consumed both shoreline and horizon, the sea spread past the edge of hope, black as a heartache.

I zipped my bag tight against the ocean-cold night. Sparks rose from our fire pit along with the scent of burning wood. An occasional snap broke through the lull of crashing surf, as the waves beat an effortless rhythm.

For a moment, the loose sand conformed to the contours of my body, before shifting beneath me. Inextricably connected to the pull of the ocean, earth gave way and left me unsupported, adjusting to find comfort.

In years to come, the ground would shift with regularity, but I was out of sync, unable to catch the rhythm.

III

Saint Louis. August.

Traffic whizzed past me, down South Grand Boulevard, too close. I kept near the buildings—family shops that butted the narrow sidewalk. Weathermen proclaimed it the hottest summer on record, but I was not discouraged. Only on foot could I lose myself in the eccentricities of my new neighborhood, and I was determined to make this neighborhood my home.

When a car engine throttled down from whiz to idle, I turned to investigate. A boat-long '70s sedan pulled within arm's reach. The driver pushed his sunglasses down the bridge of his nose, lizard eyes peering over the frames at me. *Idiot.* I walked away, and lizard-eyes sped off.

Behind every facade lay a treat: German import shop, Italian restaurant, bakery, used bookstore. Even a neighborhood market. South Grand held a place for all of them. There'd be a place for me, too.

Days later, temperatures broke. At seven a.m., eighty degrees, I seized the chance for a mile-long stroll to Tower Grove Park. A motorcycle roared between lanes as it whipped through a yellow light. The station wagon behind it screeched to a halt at the red. I turned down Magnolia, a leafy street with broad lawns that absorbed the traffic noise from Grand. Halfway down the block, I paused before jaywalking to the park on the other side. A car stopped to let me cross. I waved thank you. The driver was pursing his lips in a slow-motion kiss.

Fuck.

My heart raced, but I strolled with fake nonchalance into the park to find cover. Inside a gazebo, I sank to the floor, panting as though I'd been chased. There was an edge to the mid-morning stillness, which caused me to jump when squirrels rustled through the trees. I was desperate to get home, but how, which way? Was he waiting? I crept across the expanse of green and zigzagged through side streets.

I stopped walking for two weeks.

The temperature climbed to a hundred, but I needed eggs, and the market was only a couple of blocks away. Besides, I missed South Grand.

I reached the store just as a bus groaned to a halt, spitting riders from its maw. Inside the market's sliding doors, air conditioning turned my sweaty skin to shivers. I grabbed a cart and headed toward the dairy case, tossed in Oreos and Diet Coke along the way.

The register dinged my total, and the clerk snapped open a grocery sack. "Find everything okay, ma'am?"

"Sure did."

Overhead Diana Ross questioned, "Why do fools fall in love?"

A man lounged on the bus stop bench, skinny as a knife blade. He was leaning forward, elbows on his thighs, hands dangling between his knees. He swiveled in my direction, his flat expression trained on the spot where humidity plastered my tee shirt to my chest. I shifted the sack to cover myself, but he saw through both the bag and the shirt. Determined to keep my pace steady, I crossed in front of him, the air between us as thick as diesel fumes.

Legs trembling, I reached the corner two doors from my apartment. As I stepped off the curb in front of a car at the stop sign, a passenger poked his head out the window. "Hey, baby. Fine sister like you all alone?"

Fucking shit.

I staggered into the apartment, but its double-locked door offered no reassurance.

South Grand was not my home.

IV

Minneapolis. January.

Twenty below and too cold to snow. The streets had shrunk into narrow passes that cut through mountain ranges of drifts, blackened from exhaust smoke. The drifts were permanent features in the landscape between Halloween and April Fool's Day. I found a parking space, noted the church on the corner, and slogged half a mile to campus. Dwarfed by the three-story Greek columns of Johnston Hall, I was hopping from foot to foot just outside the glass doors. A woman on the inside, pulling on her mittens, blocked my way in. *Let me in I'm gonna die I'm gonna die*

I'm gonna die. Irritation fueled a tiny fire that lessened the chill from one square inch of my flesh. After the woman breezed by, I rushed into the lobby, where I stomped snow off my Sorels.

Climbing the stairs to the third floor, I molted. Unwound the wool scarf from over my nose and mouth. My breath had been warm and moist inside the scarf and was shocked to meet up with the chilly air. Pushed the hood off my head to rest between my shoulder blades like a cape. Plucked off earmuffs and in a single well-practiced wrist-flip, snapped them into a compact bundle, which I slipped into my coat pocket. Unsnapped then unzipped the down coat, an action made clumsy by my gloved hands. I hated to take off my gloves; my fingers still ached with cold. *Mittens. Gotta get mittens.*

One more adaptation, and I'd feel at home.

I was a grad student at the University of Minnesota, which put my mind into research mode, cracking the code of Minneapolis winters. I could write a thesis on driving skills alone: pump the brakes, don't hold them down; downshift on hills, don't brake; correct your steering less than you think you should. I learned how to plow my Honda CRX through bumper-deep slush. I adjusted my route home to test my ability to take off from a stop sign at the crest of a slippery hill. When my tires began to spin, I rolled back until the front tires found purchase. My confidence surged, and my pride, too: I'd adapted.

But my skills were merely the survival techniques of a traveler just passing through. The harder I tried, the less at home I felt. Home is the place where effort is laid to rest.

Locals, with names like Larsdatter, Helland, and Oefstedal, traced their bloodlines in rituals handed down by the tribe: ice skating, ice fishing, ice sculpting. I had enrolled in a cross-country ski class, but on the first day, fell on top of a little blond girl and never went back.

At the end of my workday in Johnston Hall, I layered up again—coat, earmuffs, hood, scarf, gloves—and walked back to my car through the early dark. The church was there. My car was not. I searched up and down the block. It must have been a different church. A different block. I ransacked my mind for clues, but *what ought to be* refused to turn into *what was*.

Back at my desk, I called the police to report my car stolen. The bored operator on the switchboard said, "Probably towed. Driver's license number?" She found me in the computer and my car at an impound lot. How would I get home? How would I get my car? How would I pay the ticket? My mind wobbled to its feet and reconstructed the scenario: that I'd noticed a church but not a half-buried pole that bore vital parking information. "Happens a lot this time of year," she said.

Gotta look harder for parking signs.

One more adaptation, and I'd feel at home.

V

Kansas City. May.

North Main Street was littered with storm debris.

Tornado sirens had wailed the night before, and I'd huddled in a bathroom, every minute at least an hour long, but no funnels had touched down.

Setting out on my morning walk, I dragged a downed limb onto the growing pile on our lawn. I pushed my long sleeves above my elbows. A chainsaw whined in the distance as I strode toward Briarcliff Greenway, a block-long swath of grass and dandelions the city kept mowed. A dust mop of a puppy bounded toward me, her brush tail slicing the air with *hello, come play*, and a young woman on the other end of her leash. I stooped to pet dust mop, but couldn't get in a good pat. She hopped and squeaked and wound her leash around my ankles, while the young woman tried to untie me. "Sorry. She's training."

Such was our routine. I knew they lived in the blue house on the corner. I knew she'd planted a stand of coreopsis in her front yard, whose yellow starbursts surprised me every summer.

Sometimes the young woman was accompanied by a toddler pushing an umbrella stroller. Once we'd met just as the retinue was starting out, and the little girl had skipped along in my blind spot. She'd peppered me with questions and her own answers, during which I'd fantasized a life-long friendship between us—taught her to read, gave her sage advice after a teenage spat with her boyfriend.

The young woman untangled the leash from my feet. I wanted to ask her name, but she and the pooch hurried past, toward their blue house on the corner, dust mop's yap yap yap fading ....

At the end of the greenway, the sidewalk u-turned into a wooded hillside, zigzagged by blacktop trails. A sign identified the network as Briarcliff Trails of Our Community. *Our community*, a paradox, a mystery.

Because the pathways climbed to an elementary school, the trees wore nametags, white cards tacked high onto the trunks: shumard oak (far from its origins on the Atlantic coastal plain, a traveler like me), sugar maple, river birch. Just in time, a glimmer warned of a spider web, which dangled from branch to ground, as wide as a man's outstretched arms. Yards away, posed on the blacktop like garden statuary—a doe. Her head lifted, black orbs trained on me.

Will it attack? Dawn, it's only a deer. Maybe the one that ate my tulips.

The deer didn't move. I didn't move.

How can a living creature be that still?

Individual hairs on her coat leaped into 3D—tan, black, white. Her impossibly opaque eyes drained the tension from my muscles. Her quiescence gentled my hummingbird mind to a soft landing on this bit of blacktop. Locked in a staring contest with a deer, I was planted firmly on the earth.

She showed no fear. Her unflinching stance telegraphed I was nothing special. Just a piece of the familiar landscape. A two-footed specimen she'd encountered often during a morning forage. I belonged.

The hair on my arms rose in response.

Facing off across the asphalt, the deer and I shared a space that required no ritual for admission other than standing still. Over the years, I'd raised great clouds of dust, flapping my angst around, trying to fit in. When the dust settled, *right here* materialized, where each creature, two-footed and otherwise, occupied its rightful corner. A robin stalked along the edge of the underbrush, perfectly at home in suburbia; after all, development had softened the soil, transforming it into an easy pathway for earthworms. The fat russet breast bobbed up and down as the robin tugged its brunch out of the ground. The spider I'd sidestepped was working its way toward a recent catch. If I had stumbled into its web, it would have made repairs efficiently and hunkered down for the next meal. Adaptation without angst.

The deer slipped into the underbrush, at ease on the pavement, at ease in the scrub. I envied her sure-footedness.

I started up the hill again, always uphill. Lost soon enough in the effort.

MAMA REVISITED

I've gotten to know Mama better since she died.

The intuitive was wearing oven mitts when she opened her front door and waved me in for a consult with my spirit guides. "I've been baking. We'll have cookies later." After Wendy and I settled on her couch, she spread Tarot cards on the coffee table. She turned them over one by one, her manicured fingernail tapping each card for emphasis.

Tarot cards? Really? Why isn't she channeling my guides?

"What?" Wendy asked.

A whiff of oatmeal cookies overpowered the candle she'd lit.

"Well. Umm. I prefer the guides."

She put the cards away and walked over to her bookcase, stood for a moment without speaking. She was emptying herself of Wendy.

When she turned to face me, the guides scolded like impatient parents. "She thinks wisdom only comes through in this fashion." "It will be hard to live up to her potential." "If she's going to be creative, she'll be destructive too."

Even though the guides were scolding me, I was finally receiving the attention I was starving for.

Wendy scrunched her face as if trying to make out an object in the distance. "They're gone now. Someone else is here." Wendy paused. "A woman who hasn't been here before. Standing in a shadow. Stoop-shouldered." Wendy was still as a corpse. "She's looking right at you, but she doesn't say anything."

I leaned forward. "Mama?"

Most days during my childhood, Mama didn't look at me. She wandered from room to room like a zombie. Rooms with roaches in the cupboards and grime on the floors. Rooms where laundry drifted in the corners. I spent a lot of time in the corner, too, wary of the zombie, wishing I had a mother. She and Dad often argued behind their closed bedroom door, while we kids eavesdropped from the top step, long past our bedtimes. One night two men escorted Mama—listless and compliant—down those stairs. I didn't know who they were, but Dad didn't try to stop them. He led them through the living room and grim-faced, held the front door open. I watched them take my mother away.

In the 1960s, no one spoke of mental illness.

Dad said Mama "got better real fast" after the doctor threatened shock treatments.

My grandmother called her lazy.

In Wendy's living room, I felt the gaze I'd craved for fifty years. "Mama's here."

Fragmented images of her that I'd long forgotten floated together in my imagination. The woman she'd surely been, in between bouts of depression, eased into the foreground. A tremor went up my arm.

"She's gone," Wendy said.

Her visit was over, but Mama had walked into my life and made it clear she'd never leave me.

The Mama I'd forgotten loved to dress up.

In my favorite picture, she posed with hands on hips, a wide grin on her face. She wore a forties skirt suit: broad shoulders, nipped waistline, and her feet clad in ankle strap peep-toes. The outfit was topped with an admiral's hat that framed her shoulder-length waves. The epitome of chic. It took a beat to realize the headgear was a joke. It belonged to Dad's kid brother Al, who was standing next to her, hatless, in his high school band uniform.

She and Dad celebrated a New Year's Eve at the Elks Club. Her outfit: a champagne-colored chiffon dress. Short puffy sleeves. Sweetheart neckline. Full skirt billowing over petticoats. They swished when she walked.

She took my brother Michael, in high school then, to a production of "The World of Suzie Wong," at Des Moines' KRNT Theatre. Her outfit: a black knit dress that hugged her hourglass figure. A narrow belt of the same fabric. Stockings with seams up the back. Black suede pumps.

Michael remembered she'd struck up a conversation with a young Asian couple sitting next to her. "What nationality are you?" (They were Japanese and had emigrated to Hawaii.) Perhaps she followed up with *Where are your parents? How did you end up in Des Moines? Do you miss Japan?* These are questions I would have asked. I inherited her curiosity, along with her depression.

My sister Michelle is a minister; part of her ministry is helping the living communicate with loved ones who have passed on. "Do you think Mama has a message for me?" I asked.

"Let's go walking in my favorite place, and I'll find out," she said.

At Santa Barbara's Botanical Garden, we found a winding path that led uphill and down, in and out of the shade. We stopped on a stone bridge to listen to a creek that gurgled underneath. As we continued, the hot sun on my bare arms turned into cool, still air. We'd entered a redwood grove.

"This is the spot," Michelle said.

We sat side by side on a bench in the shade of the giants, and then she wandered off alone. I leaned way back to see the treetops. I was a supplicant in a holy place, as I'd been at monasteries I'd visited on retreat. The redwoods silenced the chatter in my mind.

Michelle returned and sat beside me. "Mama said she's proud of you. She said keep writing. It's important."

It was a Christmas present in July.

When I was eight, she noticed I'd developed a chronic stomach-ache and insisted on taking me to the doctor, against Dad's objection. She noticed my dislike of chili. Whenever she made the dish for supper, she fried me a burger instead.

She noticed a world brought into our living room every night by Huntley and Brinkley. When her sisters visited from out of town, her conversation was peppered with words meaningless to me: Chiang Kai-shek, Roosevelt, The War.

Summers, Mama used to pore over the Burpee Seed Catalog. I sat across from her with my elbows on the kitchen table and the backs of my thighs sticking to the plastic chair seat. Mama didn't look up. Her house was dirty, her children stinky, but marigolds bloomed by the front porch.

The year I turned fourteen, Dad—divorced and remarried—moved the family to California. I don't remember saying good-bye to Mama. She wrote to me all through my high school years. I don't remember answering. She remarried. I didn't congratulate her. We exchanged neither phone calls nor visits. She died shortly after I graduated from college. I didn't go back to Des Moines for her funeral. I'd inherited her looks, but also Dad's attitude toward money. The idea of buying something as expensive as a plane ticket was alien to me. I was poor, and Mama was a stranger.

She died of heart failure.

After she visited me at Wendy's house, I suspected her heart had been broken.

My father punished us with a razor strop. Or his bare hand. A smack on the backside sent the victim airborne. It only took a glare to shrink me into submission. Surely Mama bore witness. Did he hit her, too?

Dad woke up one morning with Mama holding a gun to his head.

He told the story when we were all grown, as proof of her madness.

After she visited me at Wendy's house, I revisited that old story. I suspected she stood over him, sighting him down the barrel of that pistol, waiting. After his beady eyes opened, I imagined she said, "Don't you touch my kids again, mother fucker."

By the time we were adults, Mama's children resided in three different states, but one summer Michael, Michelle, our brother Bill, and I visited her grave together. Or rather, Bill took the rest of us. He and Mama had remained close, and after she died, he made a pilgrimage to her gravesite every year. But it was the only time the four of us had come together to honor her. Bill bent down and brushed dirt from her headstone, set flat in the ground.

I felt awkward.

Bill said, "She was happy after she remarried."

Michelle said, "She's here now."

"You mean you feel her spirit?" Michael asked.

"I see her. Right over there." She pointed to a spot behind Bill's shoulder. "Wearing a white dress. She's at peace. Happy we're here. Together."

It was then it occurred to me. How devastating to have her children wrenched away, clear across the country.

We stood in a circle around her grave, our heads bowed. We said nothing. My shoulders slumped under the weight of confusing emotions.

As we crossed the cemetery to return to the car, our steps were slow and labored in the Iowa humidity.

Michael and Michelle spent the weekend at my house in Kansas City. Michelle took to sitting alone on the patio, surrounded by pots of roses, petunias, and marigolds. I'd inherited Mama's taste for marigolds.

At dinner, amid our chatter, her gaze turned toward the dining room window. She had a way of saying big things in a small way that made the thing even bigger. "Mama was on your patio today. Now she's standing just outside the window."

I smiled to think of Mama striking a pose on my patio, all dressed up in a skirt suit and peep-toe pumps.

ON WAKING FROM A NAP

Shadows of sleep solidified into recognizable objects: ceiling fan, nightstand, bookshelf. My husband's arm lay heavy across my shoulder and chest. His breath brushed my neck. I pulled his arm tighter around me, a protest against my empty stomach's insistence I get up to make dinner.

While cicadas sang torch songs outside our bedroom window, I mapped the steps involved in making my way from bed to refrigerator. Relax grip from around Ben's wrist. Plant bare feet on the hardwood floor. Tiptoe down the hall, pause to straighten the satin wall hanging and let my palm enjoy the slip and slide of it. And then down the stairs and into the kitchen. Open the refrigerator to a rush of cold air. But why? No food to be found there equal to that of Ben's hand grazing my cheek.

For a week in late April 2015, the Kansan brood of Magicicada septemdecim tunnel to the earth's surface. In a choreographed invasion that stirs the twilight throughout Texas, Oklahoma, Missouri, Kansas, and Iowa, the periodical cicadas steal toward the nearest vertical surfaces, to which they cling overnight. They shed exoskeletons in the midday heat. After the adults fly into the treetops on brand new lacy wings, their discarded shells stick to tree trunks, light posts, mailboxes, headstones.

Winged adult cicadas dry in the sun for a day, and then sing to attract females. When flexed, tymbals—drum-like organs buried inside hollow abdomens—release a mating cacophony across the countryside and over suburban neighborhoods. Tymbals, a word reminiscent of crashing cymbals. Appropriate, because Magicicadas chorus at eighty-five decibels, as loud as a blender. Awakened to the single purpose of reproduction, males rarely even stop to eat. They collaborate as well as any orchestra; individual soloists alternate their serenades with short flights to search out receptive females. After cutting slits into tree twigs, each female deposits up to 400 eggs.

Their physical energy spent, their bodies starved, both males and females die. The corpses of Magicicada Brood IV carpet the ground.

The ceiling fan blades rotated light and dark stripes above me. I nudged the pillow into a more comfortable position, coaxing the memory foam to remember a new shape for my head. Ben's stomach pressed into my back. His midsection supported me. Lying next to him, I was relieved of the anxiety caused by navigating the world as an independent organism.

I wasn't supposed to crave support.

I had been raised during the Ms. Magazine era. Run your own company. Change your own spark plugs. Show no hint of dependence. Ms. daughters would take care of ourselves, thank you very much. Ms. daughters were trained to fly solo.

To achieve the penultimate goal of the species—reproduction—Magicicadas employ a two-pronged survival strategy.

First prong: predator satiation—1.5 million cicadas per acre of land sates the most voracious appetites. And appetites wait in abundance to be sated. Dogs and cats gorge until indigestible wings block their livers. Starlings feast, grow bloated, and cannot fly. Cicadas are high-protein food for hawks, deer, and squirrels; turtles and fish; raccoons and possums; lizards, snakes, and mice;

spiders, ants, and wasps. Even humans in Australia, Thailand, Papua New Guinea, and Japan consider cicadas a delicacy. But the sacrifice of many increases survival odds for the individual.

Second prong: out-of-sync life cycle. No bird or beast of prey can limit its diet to a food source available just once every seventeen years. Any predator with a one-year lifespan crosses paths with cicadas once every seventeen generations. Other rapacious threats are longer-lived. Black garden ants commonly live fifteen years, and red-tailed hawks can survive as long as twenty-nine. Either span will dependably intersect a Magicicada emergence, but only once in a lifetime. Thus the cicada is not essential for the existence of any single species.

I tracked a single blade of the ceiling fan as it orbited the motor, ruffling air across my ankles. The bed frame creaked as I twisted halfway onto my back, head in the crook of Ben's arm, my side pressed against his stomach. His heart thumped a lullaby that eased my spine into the mattress.

Outside our window it was spring—chirpy and pastel. Robin eggs and irises popped new life into the garden. I'd seen a sparrow hen on the ground under the feeder, placing seeds into her chick's open beak, which pointed up at her from atop a puffball body. Mourning doves fluttered and strutted around the pair, unnoticed. The hen's world was reduced to a single task: filling that upturned beak.

Snapshot. Mama and I standing side by side in a doorway, me barely as tall as her waist. She's angled away from me, leaning against the doorframe, and the negative space between us forms an upside-down triangle. Behind us, the interior of our house is shadowed. I'm as invisible to Mama as the sticky summer air. I stare into the direction she's looking, puzzling out how to become the prize in the distance that's absorbed her attention.

Snapshot. Stepmother and I strolling down the beach. Grown women, arm in arm, shoulder to shoulder. The Pacific sprays a mist against my face. At water's edge, sand squishes between my toes. My hip bumps hers. She says: "Let go. You're constricting my movements." I snatch my arm away and press it tight against my side. Of course she's right. It's easier to walk with distance between us, especially with my head bowed—me watching my step.

Snapshot. A girlfriend and I slouching on a sofa, at a party. She shouts, "Puppy pile." Before I can ask what it means, half a dozen people pile on, legs and arms splayed and overlapping. A chest bone under my head. My hand on a jeans-clad thigh, the worn denim soft under my palm. My own legs buried who-knows-where. The weight secures my limbs like rich loam holding on to tree roots. After we untangle, I feel exposed.

Last week when I emerged for a break from writing, I discovered Ben napping without me. Words had flowed freely from brain to laptop that afternoon; I had balked at interrupting a productive work session. But what if I never felt his arms around me again? What if I never again felt skin on skin, his flesh breathing sustenance into mine? The bedroom doorway framed my ambivalence. A floorboard groaned underfoot. Ben shifted, his slumber undisturbed. I crawled into bed beside him.

Nymphs hatch after ten weeks. Instinct pulls them to the edge of host branches and then drops them to the earth, where they tunnel underground, plowing through cool damp soil. As many as fifty share a hole a mere twelve inches in diameter, feeding on the sap stored in tree roots. Cicada nymphs specialize in a variety of sap that flows upward instead of downward. Because they work against gravity, their jaws are stronger than their size would suggest, heads forward of their bodies. They are bred for sucking.

As nymphs, they mature through five juvenile stages and at the end of each, shed their skins. During their seventeen-year growth cycle, they will venture only a few feet in any direction; they are completely nourished within the bulls-eye where instinct dropped them.

The ceiling fan receded into shadow as late afternoon dimmed our east-facing bedroom to a half-light. Bunched under my knees, the sheets were scratchy, a brand I'd bought on sale. I lay on my back, pressing tight against Ben, and in his sleep, his arms encircled me. The heat that radiated from his skin warmed mine. A faint scent of shampoo enticed me to stroke his baby-fine hair. My stomach rumbled, but I felt no need to obey its demand. I was nourished lying next to my husband, in the bed where instinct had drawn me.

TANGO FOR FRANKIE

The August heat squeezed between my husband and me like the third person on a date. Holding hands and sipping Cokes, we plodded through our annual visit to the state fair. We trudged through the barns and the pens. Climbed on tractors, looked at cows and then sheep. Humidity glued tee shirts to midsections, defeating our efforts to conceal muffin top and paunch. Comfort trumped dignity on state fair days – it laid bare spidery veins, wrinkly knees, and wiggly arms.

Ben held his ice-filled cup against his forehead. "Ready for the goats? They're next up."

A bead of sweat traced a path down my nose.

"No. Let's find some A.C."

"Right behind you, Puddin' Cake." He patted my rear, and I was twenty again, that magical age before gravity got personal.

We slipped into the nearest building with glass double doors, not caring what might lurk inside. Cold air blasted us. We soaked it up for a moment and then drifted toward a nearby crowd.

Ben grabbed my arm. "Watch out."

I sidestepped a tortoise the size of a hassock. It retreated into its shell, leaving only the point of its snout visible … and leaving me wondering what on earth it was doing there.

We edged closer to the front. A pre-teen boy held court behind a conference-sized table. A terrarium on the table was crawling with tree frogs the color of lime sherbet. The boy reached in and offered the frogs to the crowd, like hors d'oeuvres.

He held one in my direction.

"Okay," I said. "Maybe if I do this I won't scream the next time a toad shows up while I'm weeding."

"Yeah, he'll just sit in your hand." He placed the cute little critter in my palm. The frog, unaware of the rules, crept toward my elbow.

"Oh, no. Oh, no. It's moving. I feel its claws."

"Lady, hold your arm level, and he'll sit still."

I did. The frog did not. It headed toward my face, onto which, if I didn't take evasive action, it would spew chartreuse slime that would have to be removed with Ben's power sander.

My voice climbed an octave – "It's still going" – for every centimeter the demon scaled. "Get it off!"

Somebody screamed. I couldn't tell if it was the frog or me. But boy rescued beast just in time to save it from a lethal dousing of Coke.

Onlookers smirked. Ben nudged me toward a neighboring table. Five-gallon jars sat on top of it, with signs attached. Mexican Redkneed Tarantulas. Hissing Cockroaches from—.

"Good Lord!"

At the far end of the table, a man chatted with spectators, while a massive snake—an eight-foot albino boa constrictor, according to a nearby sign—twisted itself around his outstretched arms.

A woman standing next to me pointed to the boa. "Is it poisonous?"

"No, no. Do you want to hold her?"

Do you want *her* to hold *you* would have been more accurate.

The woman shook her head and jumped back, stepping on my foot and crashing into three teenaged girls. Laughter rippled through the audience.

I sympathized with that poor lady. One childhood summer, a fifth-grade bully named Frankie had terrorized me with the garter snakes that slithered around our neighborhood. Leaping from behind a lilac bush, Frankie would throw a writhing serpent at me, then laugh and run away. Because snakes were plentiful—and Frankie persistent—I hated that summer.

Since then, fear of snakes launched by fifth-grade boys had matured into mid-life anxieties. I was afraid of turning the wrong way onto a one-way street. I was afraid of absentmindedly walking into the men's restroom. I was afraid of standing in the express line with too many items in my cart. I longed to be brave, to sweep in on a white stallion and rescue myself. But I was afraid of horses.

The man inside the boa surveyed his audience, and I tried to disappear by studying my shoes. The strategy failed, as it had in eleventh-grade geometry whenever I hadn't known the answer.

The teacher looked right at me. "How about you? Do you want to hold her?"

"Me?"

Without permission, my head nodded *yes*. My stomach countered, *Are you crazy?*

The snake charmer moved in my direction. "Come on around to this side of the table."

"You gonna do it?" Ben asked.

"I don't know."

What? I could *not* have said that, because I most certainly *did* know that I would *not* do it.

But … on the other hand. A coward dies a thousand deaths. I had nothing to fear but fear itself. Today was the first day of the rest of my life, dammit.

My mutinous left foot took a step. *Me? Hold a snake, on purpose?*

"Maybe," I said to Ben. The right foot joined the mutineer. "Yeah."

He pried the Coke from my hand. "Terrific. I'll hold your cup."

I walked around the table (giving a wide berth to the hissing roaches) until I was face-to-face with the man and eyeball-to-eyeball with the snake.

"Hold your arms straight out at your sides."

I stood like a scarecrow.

The man unwound the boa from his chest and arms. With one hand under its head and the other supporting its midsection, he draped the sinewy reptile across my shoulders.

"Be still," he said.

No problem. The snake felt smooth and cool. Of the two of us, I was the clammy one. It lay across my shoulders, no doubt bored by just another day at work. I was sorry I'd ever gotten out of bed and certainly regretted passing up the goats.

The boa weaved and wound its way along my shaking limbs, reptilian muscles rippling as it explored the wobbly terrain. The coils gripped like steel cables, and my outstretched arms ached with the effort of keeping the weight aloft. I gritted my teeth, clenched my fists, and contemplated the void, while the serpentine body wrapped around me. A casual squeeze would have snuffed my tiny flame.

I can't believe Ben let me do this.

The outside of me froze, while the inside quivered. Heart raced and temples pulsed. My palms were sweating like a cold bottle of beer, and my mouth was as dry as granola without any milk, and the butterflies in my stomach were quaking as they flew.

Then the boa flicked her tongue.

With that flash of movement, the sense of weight on my shoulders receded. Motion took the foreground. Threatening mass morphed into shape-shifting mercury.

An imprisoned breath escaped my lips. I saw Ben giving me a thumbs-up, and then I turned my head slightly to get a better look at the creature I was wearing.

The boa slipped and glided. She undulated around my arms in a liquid dance, controlling me with the grace of a tango partner. A ginger widow's peak branched into delicate honeycombs that wrapped her creamy skin in a mantle of lace. As she loosened and tightened her embrace, flecks of gold from nose to tail flirted with the dappled sunlight in the room.

Yet, at the same time, her smoldering power emboldened me. It incinerated all pretense of reticence. It destroyed any notion of decorum. Blazed away the remains of afraid. I was Wonder Woman, vanquishing my foes after bouncing their impotent bullets off my bracelets.

Muscle fatigue finally overtook my craving to prolong the moment. Mouthing a silent thank you, I nodded my readiness to be released. With her keeper's assistance, the boa unwound herself from my shoulders and returned to his. She flicked her tongue three times, and then she settled.

I strutted back around the table, hands on my hips.

Ben punched the air with his fist. "Yes!"

"Wow ... that was ... well ... " I pursed my lips, searching for the words until the desire to speak slipped away on a sigh. I grinned, danced a little jig, and kissed my sweetheart.

"Honey," he said, "you just earned yourself a corndog." He draped his arm around my shoulders, handing me the Coke.

After we stepped outside, I cast a longer shadow in the afternoon sun. My stride lengthened. Under the steamy summer sky, my cool was impermeable.

Frankie never would have touched that boa.

GOOD BONES

After an hour of wisdom from other dimensions, I wondered how I'd been so silly as to believe in such nonsense as gravity or arithmetic. While I sat in her living room, enthralled, Wendy read Tarot cards, threw the I Ching, and channeled the voices of mystical guides. The guides laughed a deep-throated laugh that made me feel like a little girl they loved to indulge. Of course they would indulge me—one of them was Mother Kim, who had died ten years earlier. As my session with Wendy ended, she issued a final instruction. "Buy her purple irises for Mother's Day."

Dad married Kim Carol Reed when I was twelve. In my stoic and despondent eyes, she looked like a movie star: lips stained crimson, fingernails pink. She dressed in lilac, violet, and amethyst. My clothes were unwashed gray, my hair uncombed. I avoided mirrors. And people too, preferring the comfort of loneliness to the company of playmates.

Mother Kim and Dad bought a house, and before moving the family in, they painted the dining room red. The house they'd moved us out of hadn't been painted anything, its dust-covered interior a faded shade of poverty. The new dining room was as warm and hypnotic as a fireplace. I'd sit alone at the table, pretending to read, the room's incandescence a beacon. The year we lived in that house, Mother Kim nudged me out of isolation. She enrolled me in ballet. I went roller-skating with my Sunday school class and joined the mixed chorus at junior high.

In high school, she introduced me to Vogue, which occupied a spot on her nightstand beside a bottle of Chanel No. 5. She pointed out bold patterns on bright fabrics, but I wanted to hide from the colors she admired.

When I was sixteen, she handed me a Robinson's Department Store shopping bag. Under the tissue paper, I found a hot-pink party dress, a slender column of knife pleats, lined in satin. A pleated lampshade with spaghetti straps. I held it up—pinkies extended, eyebrow lifted, lips pooched.

"Oh, for heaven's sake, just try it on."

I pulled the dress on over my shorts.

Mother Kim's expression softened as she pushed me in front of a mirror. "Very pretty. See for yourself."

She made me wear it for a cocktail party she and Dad were giving. I squirmed through the evening, but years later I would surprise myself, remembering the softness in her eyes and the slide of a satin lining against my skin.

Mother Kim was also clairvoyant, reporting that lost souls were fluttering down the hall, or some far-flung relative was in trouble. As a teenager, I found it annoying. She knew when I'd sneaked off to school in a too-short skirt. She berated me for attracting unwanted attention, but mini-skirts were the uniform of 1969, the camouflage that allowed me to disappear. As an adult preoccupied with marriage and career, I found her ESP guilt-inducing. More often than not, my phone rang just as it crossed my mind to call her, and I imagined reproach in her hello. But her clairvoyance worked under my awareness, cracking reality, calling me eventually to Wendy's mystical counsel.

I paused before pulling out of Wendy's driveway. Why had she suggested purple irises? She didn't know my stepmom's favorite color had been purple. And I couldn't recall Mother Kim mentioning a fondness for irises.

Oh, well. There were other things to think about. At fifty-something I was on my own, newly divorced, and in the market for a house.

My realtor, Sue, was waiting for me in the parking lot of her office. We climbed into her sedan. I'd seen so many houses, they'd blurred in my memory by the time she pulled into the driveway of a brick split-level with white shutters. The brick felt homey, the shutters welcoming. Sue led the way up the stairs to the stoop. She stopped for a second, as though listening. "I have a good feeling about this." Something Mother Kim often said.

I peeked in the front door. "Oh, my."

At the end of an entry hall, the kitchen glowed orange as a clown's wig. Ceiling and walls. The orange was intensified by sunlight streaming in through the windows. I was aghast. It was a color that mocked good taste and broke rules. Such a color would only lead to mischief. I closed my eyes, then opened them again. The orange sprang to life. I couldn't help laughing, like the first time cranking a jack-in-the-box, until "Pop! Goes the weasel."

Sue pointed out the sink and countertops needed replacing, and the subflooring was visible through holes in the linoleum.

Throughout the house, we encountered design inspired by a 64-pack of crayons. Banana in the family room. Powder blue in the nursery. In a second bedroom, color divided the walls horizontally, raspberry from windowsill to ceiling (across the ceiling, too), blueberry from midline to floor (inside the closet, too). How could a sane person think those colors were compatible? Who could sleep in here? Who would do this to a room? Bunk beds. Children slept in here. A mother indulging her daughters would do this to a room, that's who.

Sue scowled and strode into the hallway. "Awful colors. Beige sells."

I lingered in the bedroom. Attached to one wall was a munchkin's full-length mirror, the top of it level with my waist. I knelt in front of it. The walls, reflected behind me, said yes. *Of course you can have pink. Blue too, if you want.* Said yes to a twelve-year-old. *A red dining room will keep you safe.* Spoke to a teenager who avoided mirrors. *Yes, you are pretty. See for yourself.*

I caught up with Sue downstairs as she opened the back door. The patio bore the hallmarks of a place well played-in, where children had just been whisked away by parents in a hurry. A turquoise three-wheeler had crashed head-on into the retaining wall that surrounded the terrace. A red wagon was parked nearby. On its side lay a bicycle with a hot pink basket between the handlebars, the shade reminiscent of my long-ago party dress.

A playhouse stood in the middle of the yard. The girls must have sat beneath the red roof, fussing at their dolls. Had I ever fussed at dolls? Sue was kicking the earth near the fence line. "Looks like they used to have a vegetable garden." Flowers, too. In beds that bordered the yard on three sides, the leaves of spring bulbs were just breaking ground.

I followed Sue through the banana family room on our way to the basement. In the cool of the cellar, she patted a steel beam. "The house has settled, but they've reinforced it well." She nodded, more to herself than me. "It's got good bones." Construction, location, and price met with her approval. She'd negotiate for a kitchen remodel.

I grinned. My own house.

Sunday evening before escrow closed, I stole into the back yard. Weeds had overrun the lawn since the owners had moved out. Chives from the vegetable garden had invaded the grass, which looked awfully brown. The playhouse was gone, only its concrete slab remaining. What had I done? I couldn't possibly afford to replace that cement with turf. Couldn't afford to buy new countertops. New kitchen floor. Paint over all those garish colors. Me, Ms. Levelheaded, enchanted by a child's bedroom.

The house I was moving from hadn't sold yet, not even a nibble. On top of everything else, I had two house payments. The arithmetic defied my checkbook. Sue said she'd had a good feeling about this place, but maybe she'd simply taken advantage of a naïve buyer.

This was the only mortgage I'd signed alone.

The decision mine.

The failure mine.

I sat down hard on a stone bench. As I rubbed my temples to conjure up reassurance, something rustled at the rear of the yard, a flash of color.

The bulbs had bloomed. Purple irises were swaying in the breeze along the back fence … and in the bed beside the patio … and down the length of the property line.

Buy her purple irises.

I leaned back, disbelieving and believing all at once. The irises towered over the lawn. Crabgrass shriveled, and my spine straightened. Mother Kim's favorite color coaxed me out of my doubts, as she had done for a young girl. Even though I was sitting on a concrete bench in the back yard of my new house, my house, the slide of a satin lining brushed my skin, and I realized it was Mother's Day.

THE CLEANING WOMEN

My question required sidling up to, the way a maid would ask for a day off. The conversation would be chancy with the white women milling around the yoga studio putting away their props. I could not risk the word *housekeeper*—colored girls in head rags crowded in on the word, mopping, scrubbing, and taking home leftovers. If I broached the subject head-on, these friends-for-now would know by the set of my mouth that I'd been on hands and knees on a white woman's kitchen floor. Their expressions would say that was the proper order of things.

Pottery Barn catalog in hand, I sagged onto my couch and put my feet up on the coffee table. When I pushed aside a star-shaped basket, it left a five-pointed dust-free spot. I looked away, but a cobweb strand denounced me, dangling from the middle of the ceiling to a yoga mat unfurled on the floor. Crumbs reproached my bare feet, and the odor of last night's fish-fry skillet indicted my nose.

Get off your lazy butt and clean this place.

I dropped the catalog. Who was I to own monogrammed sheets? Linen napkins would refuse delivery to my address. Silk throw pillows would insist the UPS driver take them up the hill where rich white women hired help.

In the 1940s my grandmother Mon (she'd have me tell you that rhymes with sun) cleaned for white ladies. She spoke of them with

37

fondness and gave up housework only when a better job came along: high school custodian. Better because it included a pension, and the paychecks were regular.

My Mon, a janitor? She owned a grand piano. Black and shiny, it held court in her formal living room—not to be confused with the informal sitting room just off the front porch. Mon's long brown fingers flew over the keys as she taught me to play "Clair de Lune." A ruby-hued velvet couch, its back a graceful curve, sat against one wall. An expanse of fleur-de-lis-patterned carpet swept across the room to matching chairs on the far side.

My grandmother, a maid? She owned two sets of flatware. Stainless steel in the drawer for everyday, and silver stored inside a wooden chest for Easter and Christmas. Her closets were stuffed with pretty things. Orderly rows of dresses, ankle-strap high heels along the floor, and a fox wrap draped around a hanger.

My grandmother? Scrubbed toilets? Glass bricks formed a wall behind a breakfast nook in her kitchen. When I was a little girl I sat there watching dappled sunlight play on the table, crunching bacon strips she'd set on my plate. She would rest the skillet on an iron trivet—one of a dozen that appeared whenever a hot pan threatened a counter. And on her screened-in front porch—an apple green glider that I set in motion with my big toe, while wind chimes sang to me like angels.

Weekends at Mon's house were a respite from real life.

Real life lived in Mama's house. No glider on our front porch. Instead: peeling paint, squeaky floorboards, and a razor strop, which hung by the front door. In real life, the kitchen floor was stamped with footprints ground in by muddy boots. In real life, Mama scuffed around in a shapeless housedress and used-to-be-pink slippers.

Our golden retriever lived in the basement, and even though my brother shoveled droppings off the concrete floor every day, he could never shovel away the stink. When Mama cooked chitlins, the stench clung to walls and furniture and the back of my throat. The smell was almost as bad on the days she boiled mustard greens.

On one of those mustard-greens days, while I was playing on my bedroom floor, a dark shape, antenna waving, inched up the inside of my blouse. I screamed, batted at my chest, tore off the blouse, and flung it across the room. I stomped a wad of covers that had fallen off the bed, in case more roaches were hiding in the folds. With all the strength in my skinny arm, I hurled a shoe at the window. The crash of shattering glass was both a shock and a comfort. Why couldn't I live at Mon's?

I was in high school, living with Dad halfway across the country, when I learned Mama cleaned houses too. She rode the bus to and from the suburbs along with the other help. I learned it in the nebulous way that family stories enter one's consciousness. I knew Mama cleaned for white ladies, but didn't want to know it. Especially since she became a maid the same year I realized the provenance of Mon's silver. The set in the pretty wooden box had been a cast-off from one of the women Mon cleaned for. *Give the dull knives to the colored woman, or toss them in the trash. Makes no difference.*

When I learned the truth about Mon's silver, my admiration crusted over into shame.

But by then, the high school years, self-hatred was already crawling up my skin like a roach. *Not good enough* caused me to be reserved, which the girls at my new school mistook for haughtiness. Black girls shouted, "High yellow bitch." I didn't understand "high yellow," but "bitch" was clear enough. Perhaps I began turning inward earlier, at fourteen, in American history class. On the day we studied slavery, attention leaned in my direction, the other students sneaking a peek at the only black kid in class. While the teacher droned on about half-naked girls on the auction block, I felt the sideways eyes of my classmates determining my price.

After taking an early retirement, I worked part-time assisting seniors who lived independently. One of my clients needed help tidying up her tiny apartment, a mindless chore that appealed to me after decades of climbing the corporate ladder. I liked this soft-spoken white woman the instant she invited me in, with a wave of her hand and an offer of candy from a dish on the coffee table. Such a grandma thing to do. She explained the only way to clean floors was on all fours, an opinion my own experience validated; but as soon as my knees hit the tile, I was seething. *You've got a master's degree, Dawn. What the hell are you doing on this woman's kitchen floor?* I wanted nothing more than to strangle this sweet grandma, and the women who'd given my grandmother gifts, and the women who'd hired my mother, and every other white woman who'd hired help.

I picked up the Pottery Barn catalog and dropped it into the recycle bin in my kitchen. My weariness ground footprints into the linoleum, and the footprints led to shame, and the shame circled back to weariness, which led to chitlins stinking up my peace of mind.

I wanted to live in a house like Mon's, but Mama's was the one I deserved.

When my want nudged past my inadequacy, I Googled "cleaning services in Kansas City." Sifting through the list turned out to be one more chore too big for me to start.

The search had to be narrowed. I'd have to ask someone. The women in my writers' group lived in apartments. My book group?

The same. Yoga? My age. Homeowners. A few had grown into what I dared label friends. How long would that last if any of them had actually hired a housekeeper … although nobody used that word anymore. Well then, if they'd hired a cleaning service. If they were that well off … although one was a policeman's wife, and another lived in a house smaller than mine, and another was paying for her mother's nursing home. None of them was rich. Still … it would be risky to talk with white women about cleaning houses, and if they recommended their cleaning service …

Jesus, don't let them say, "You'll love her."

Like the acquaintance who had been excited to introduce me to an artist he'd discovered. "Such an inspiration. You'll love him." Like the colleague who'd recommended an author. "Reminds me of you. You'll love her." Thrilled, foolish, each time I clicked the mentioned website. The artist was black. The author, too. And I was the black writer-friend. I waited for the next betrayal.

Four of us straggled after yoga class, always the same four, unwilling to leave each other's company just yet. My lingering was mixed with hesitation, while I waited for a wisp of courage.

I rolled my mat a turn. "Lynn, you teach all day …," I patted the edges even. "… yard's gorgeous." I rolled another turn. "How do you keep up your house?"

"Don't," she said.

Dee shoved a bolster into the corner. "Me neither."

Marilyn was at the check-in desk, flipping through an index file, for the card that bore her name. "Clean house? Give up my two-hour walks? Oh, hell, no. I deserve time for myself."

I chuckled, pretending to understand "I deserve."

In the language of my upbringing, words that followed *deserve* were: *to be taken down a notch.* Or: *a good smack.* Or: *a week in your room.* While the syllables were arranging themselves into words, and the words were lining up into a comprehensible sentence, Dee said, "I don't feel like it anymore."

I stopped breathing.

Weekends at Mon's, I had made my bed in the morning and put toys away before supper. If you didn't feel like putting the toys away, she didn't feel like letting you play with them again. Did she have feelings about cleaning her house? There were no dirty dishes after she fixed my bacon. The Steinway always gleamed, bench slid underneath, sheet music tucked inside. *The Ottumwa Courier* was the only item allowed out of place, tossed on the foot of her daybed after she worked the crossword puzzle.

I forced a breath deep into my chest. "Dee, your house is spotless. Mine's a mess."

She and Marilyn said, "Sarah."

I waited for *you'll love her.*

My apprehension drowned out most of the conversation. Snippets sneaked in. "Knows about birds." "Goes to yoga." "Like being around her."

I gulped. "How often does she come?"

"Set your own schedule."

Hire help. Set the schedule. The power was heady, yet fraught with hazard. Let a stranger into my space, which was so cluttered with self-criticism?

Dee plucked her phone from her purse. "I'm texting you her number."

Sarah came by to work out an estimate. I opened the door to greet her, and my shoulders eased when I saw she was white. I studied her face for any slight raise of an eyebrow that would betray hesitation at cleaning a black woman's house.

She had eyes for only the work. She studied grime with a professional detachment—her pace deliberate through the kitchen, bedrooms, and bathrooms. As though wearing white gloves, she brushed the frame of a Van Gogh print above my bed. "I'll dust the tops of picture frames for you." *Starry Night* had long ago disappeared from my awareness, but it could not hide from Sarah. It was harboring her enemy—dirt. She paused in the hallway to admire a Tibetan thangka. "Pretty wall hanging."

I tagged along behind her, a little girl who'd just acquired a fairy godmother. Happy energy swirled in her wake like fireflies around the hem of her gown. Windows were magically thrown open as she passed. Dust bunnies hopped away smiling.

Her presence was a cross breeze airing out my musty insecurities.

Back in the kitchen, she glanced into the back yard. "See that little black bird out by your fence? It's a junco. He'll poke around under your feeder if you sprinkle sunflower seeds on the ground."

We agreed on a price and then scheduled the job. Mon's trivets, hanging on the wall above my stove, supervised the transaction.

Sarah hugged me goodbye. "Gotta go do my house now."

Clean mine. Clean hers. It was all the same to her, a task to be checked off her list. A client to be added to her customer base. "See you next week."

A white woman was going to clean my house. Mon and Mama chuckled at the notion. Their white ladies chuckled too, because I had hired help—just as they had. My yoga classmates would chuckle in bemusement that *help* was anything other than a solution to a problem. What's the fuss? Dirty house? Call Sarah.

I brushed the nap of my velvet couch. Discovered in an antique store, it might have been a shoestring relative of Mon's sofa, which she had bought with money earned from housework. A cobweb sneaked across the baseboard. (Sarah would make short work of it.) Relaxing in a rocking chair, I wondered if Mama and Mon would have liked fairy godmothers, too. My big toe set the chair in motion—the rhythmic squeak of floor boards like an angel's song.

Sarah hadn't asked where I'd gotten that wall hanging she'd admired. She'd acted as though its hanging there was perfectly normal. As if I deserved my pretty things.

DEATH OF AN EX

G and I were sitting beside each other on a marriage counselor's couch. The counselor asked, "What do you love about Dawn?"

I turned toward my husband, toward the adoration assumed in the question.

G twisted his mustache. "Come on. That's not fair. Of course I love her. I just can't think right now."

If I had moved, my body would have shattered into pieces, the shards tinkling as they fell to the floor.

Some couples discern each other's thoughts, which are written in a language known only to them. They answer questions simultaneously. I'd read in a pop-psychology book such couples seek therapy only to repair a temporary disruption in their lines of communication, perhaps caused by a financial disaster or the death of a child. The therapist helps them find a way through their grief to re-establish the original pair bond.

We were not one of those couples.

G had inherited thick wavy hair from his Hungarian father and fluent French from his Belgian mother, traits that charmed his female employees, who fluttered unnoticed around him. After he hired me, I fell in love with his tight white jeans.

He took me to hear the blues in a smoky bar where oversized speakers crowded an undersized dance floor. The soloist kissed the mic while trumpets, keyboard, and drums pounded a throbbing beat. A couple swayed in a dim corner, her fingers intertwined loosely behind his neck and his hands resting low on her hips. Pelvis spoke to pelvis in a secret language.

The singer's mournful tone quivered up my spine. In my mind, I was swaying in the shadows, too, G's hands pressing palm prints into my hips. I danced in my chair in anticipation of him leading me onto the dance floor. He drummed on the table and kept time with thumps that sent tremors through a puddle of beer, his chair angled away from mine, the back of his head in my peripheral vision. As he bounced with the music, and I flirted with the possibility of him, our shoulders brushed. I held mine against his for a beat.

We sat through the fast numbers and then through the slow ones. I knew right then his attention would always be riveted to music other than mine, but the blues drowned out my intuition. I stirred the wine in my plastic glass.

Blues bars bled into after-work coke-enhanced parties. Dating the boss, doing coke. Finally part of the in-crowd. A late bloomer rebelling in my thirties, I was giddy.

I convinced G we might as well get married.

He agreed. "I won't do better than you."

I waited to hear *because you're my soul mate.*

The morning after he met my folks, I phoned Mother Kim. "He's nice, isn't he?" I waited to hear *I want you to be happy, because you're my favorite child.*

The silent judging phone burned my ear. I twisted a lock of hair. *Fuck. Her. She does not decide who I should marry.*

Hell, no.

I decided, even though I knew exactly what Mother Kim had witnessed in her brief encounter with him. His posture set like a salesman wooing a client. His face had lacked the softness that would reassure a parent that the man in her living room has loved her daughter for lifetimes. As I held the phone, the scene in our living room played in my mind on a painful loop. With my eyes wide shut, I could see my future unhappiness unfurl like a carpet.

We held the wedding in the home of one of his employees. The company had transferred him to another city; his new employees were strangers to me. I felt awkward, in a corner by myself, juggling a plate of snacks and a flute of champagne, but awkward felt normal.

The party eddied around me. Guests were having a raucous good time, including a woman in a fedora sitting on a couch beside G. With her hand on top of his. My gut sprang to attention. In my imagination, I marched over, removed the brazen hand, and wedged myself between The Fedora and my husband. In real life, I told myself the hands meant nothing. I stuffed outrage, then shame, and assumed the composure of a gracious bride. The Fedora and I exchanged smiles. I watched her watching me, her hand unmoving, her legs crossed. G had his back to her. He was joking with a buddy from the old days—as disconnected from the woman under the fedora as he was from me.

I knew right then buddies would command his loyalty more than I would, but someone shouted it was time to open presents. I downed another glass of champagne and took my place beside G, opening gag gifts and laughing till I cried.

I moved into his apartment, which he'd filled with collections: blues albums, metaphysical books, and Oriental rugs. The books bore opaque titles like *Spiritual Materialism* and *Wake Up and Roar.* Their pages were soft from use. I wished he read me as studiously as he read his books. Or as carefully as he read his rugs. He loved to explain knots per inch and how variations in surface coloration reflected the dye lots available to nomadic tribes. On his knees, he rubbed his hand across the pile of a prayer rug. Had he explored my skin, he would have learned a fingertip on my breastbone would melt me into surrender. He would have learned lips on my forehead would do the same, but he reserved his exploration for the rug.

We entertained ourselves frequently enough to dull the ache that settled in the back of my throat. An afternoon shopping. We were simultaneously smitten by the come-hither emerald sheen of a velvet couch in the back of an antique store. We sank into the sofa's overstuffed cushions, my fingers brushing his as we caressed the silken nap. We bought the couch, and for that afternoon at least, we were kindred spirits.

Etta James in concert. She moaned "… feel like sugar on the floor." I twisted my wedding band with my thumb, as I reached for G's hand. For that night at least, a singer's heartache drowned out mine.

A cabin on Lake Superior. We hiked all day and gobbled down platter-sized trout in local restaurants. For a weekend at least, we were buddies.

Stevie Ray Vaughn live at the Fabulous Fox Theatre. I bought a black skirt that snugged my aerobics-muscled rear, a sequined tee that outlined breasts perked from curls with twenty-pound weights, and burgundy boots on high stacked heels that turned my walk into a strut. A spritz of Shalimar.

G said, "You look nice."

I winced.

Nice. He spoke in efficient monosyllables, while I craved honeyeyed verses that took their time.

I knew right then he'd always say *nice*, but I walked through the door he held open.

We shared housekeeping, and I fantasized we shared something deeper, a nesting instinct like eagles mated for life. While Otis

Redding crooned about the tide rolling away, G swept a cotton cloth across the dining room table, caressing lemon oil into oaken contours. I emptied the dishwasher, feeling like I'd caught him with another woman. He watered plants, listening to John Lee Hooker wail about unrequited love, while I fixed dinner, unrequited in the kitchen.

In our eighteenth year of marriage, chronic back pain forced him into retirement. He became addicted to Oxycontin. Coke and pot had been party drugs, and the party had always ended when we went back to real life on Monday. Oxycontin was now his real life.

His mood swung from falling asleep mid-sentence to driving eighty through the neighborhood. He was in and out of rehab. I was in and out of a fantasy, where things returned to normal.

I found a new therapist and asked how I could be supportive through G's treatment and recovery. Ten minutes into our first session, the counselor pointed his index finger at my third eye. "How long are you going to stay in this loveless marriage?"

I froze.

The facts revealed themselves like a set of keys I'd misplaced and then discovered right in my hand.

I'm in a loveless marriage.

I can leave.

I *will* leave.

I got the velvet couch in the divorce.

G pressed for a post-marriage friendship. I pushed back. He was too closely associated with the spineless creature I used to be. To make friends with him, I'd have to make friends with her.

My temples throbbed whenever she wormed her way into my consciousness. How much had she hated herself, to have imposed an eighteen-year sentence of neglect, jealous of the rug G walked on? She was a coward. Escape was the only way to deal with her.

I took up eating and gained twelve pounds.

I took up meditation. Judgments about the coward swarmed through my mind like red ants.

I took up yoga. Week after week after week, I crashed out of tree pose. My teacher said, "Balance is all about your core." I had no core. My center failed.

I gained three pounds.

In meditation, contemplation was interrupted by interrogation—the questions like field mice that hid under rocks and then darted into the dangerous light. *Why is the coward still plaguing me? When will she disappear? Will she disappear?*

In yoga, my teacher introduced us to handstand. "It's fun," she said. "I'll hold you up. Who wants to try?" I hung back and then berated myself for timidity.

I lost two pounds.

In meditation, the teacher said, "Pay attention to sensations in your body." Roiling analysis produced the sensation that my hair was on fire. But once, between flash points of pain, a breeze blew through my mind, cooling self-reproach by a degree.

In yoga, my teacher challenged me into new poses. The world went askew when I arched into backbend, the top of my head near the floor, my tender underbelly exposed and unprotected.

I gained nine pounds.

At a meditation retreat, we learned to send kind thoughts through the ether—mental telegraph messages to a stranger, to a friend, and to a foe. I had been estranged from the sad younger me. I'd considered her a coward, simply because she had been unhappy. Stranger, friend, and foe: They were aspects of myself. I sent kind thoughts to each of us.

In yoga, we learned eagle pose. Balanced on one foot, right leg wound around left leg, arms wound around each other, and hands in prayer position, I was twined around myself. An embrace. I squeezed my gut. The center held.

I had been afraid long before G had slipped a gold band on my finger, long before I'd slipped one on his. He hadn't caused my unhappiness; our lifelines had simply intersected. It was time to acknowledge his humanity out loud.

I called him.

He said, "I'm surprised to hear from you. Thought you were pissed."

"No. There are so many things I appreciate about you. You gave me music. Robert Cray before he got famous. Stevie Ray Vaughn. I never heard sounds like that. When you sent me *Spiritual Materialism*, I read it so many times, it fell apart."

"That means a lot to me."

It meant a lot to me, too. To say those things and mean them.

I called again a year later, when I caught the final chords of an Etta James song on the radio.

"Hi. It's Dawn."

"Hey, man. Who'ziss?"

"Dawn."

"Goddammit. What an asshole to not know your voice. S'fucked up, man."

His harshness echoed my own voice, calling my younger self a coward. Was G as self-critical as I was?

"You okay?" I asked.

"I'm a junkie. Always have been."

The inevitability caught me by surprise. "I'm sorry." I said. The way you're sorry when you learn a friend has cancer.

Through the eighteen years of our marriage, G had risen from promotion to promotion, never late to work, never absent. He'd managed his savings like a financier and retired with plenty. Yet he could not escape this slurred conversation at age seventy-five. He carried the junkie inside him like an aberrant cancer cell.

I pictured him—it seemed centuries ago—nodding out at our kitchen table. The image widened to include my younger self, grim-faced and ramrod straight in a chair beside him. Unworthy of a husband who didn't nod out. Since birth, my DNA had pulled me inexorably to that kitchen table. I was a junkie for not-good-enough.

The phone grew warm, my palm moist.

On G's end, a clatter and then muffles, before the phone got back into range. He asked, "What's goin' on?"

"Just checking on you," I said.

Coughs punctuated sentences that trailed off into labored breathing. He hung up. He called back. "Anthony?" he said.

"No, this is Dawn."

He was powerless over his affliction, as I had been powerless over mine.

It seemed unlikely G would live much longer, whether he succumbed to an overdose or to a heart attack. I wanted to pay last respects at his funeral when the time came, but how do you say *let me know when you die*?

"Glad you —," he said.

I waited for more, suspended in a space where the conversation ends while the connection remains open.

A neighbor discovered his body.

Cleaning out his apartment, she gathered old photos for me (coke-fueled parties before we were married, company parties after) and stuffed them in a folder. At home, the folder on my lap, I settled onto the couch, my hand absently smoothing the velvet.

My fingertip circled a pin-sized hole where an ember from G's Marlboro had fallen. Quarters had been found between these cushions; they'd heaved up misplaced keys, and once a gift tag from a ring G had bought me. It had fit right out of the box—he knew my size. The couch cared for my misplaced treasures until I was ready to reclaim them.

PART II
Rituals

IMPERMANENCE

I stepped through the door of the meditation hall and added my shoes to the growing pile. In the crowded entryway, I bumped heads with a woman wearing a neon orange tracksuit, mouthed a 'scuze me, and moved on.

It was the first day of a ten-day retreat, led via videotape by a popular Indian teacher (hereafter referred to as "PI Teacher"). The interior walls of a ranch house had been removed to create a space big enough to squeeze in a hundred meditators, males and females separated by a center aisle.

A raised platform ran the length of the room along one wall. Zafus and zabutons formed well-disciplined rows on the floor in front of it, reserved for veterans of PI Teacher's previous courses. Behind them, heaps of sofa cushions, folded blankets, and floor pillows comprised the newbie section. Chairs lined the back wall, for those of us too inflexible to sit on the floor. Every spot bore a card with a student's name on it.

I claimed my assigned chair and tucked a shawl under my feet.

In previous years, I'd performed that ritual countless times in a meditation hall where my sangha met. I relished the routine of silent retreats. The familiar rustle as we each settled into a not-quite-comfortable position. Our teacher, attired in khakis and polo, greeting us with a gentle, "Good evening, friends." On the first night, he usually led us in an abbreviated twenty-minute sit and sent us—travel weary—off to bed. The real work started on the second day. Meditation from sunrise to moonrise (blessedly silent, except for the warble of tree frogs). Breaks for meals. Evening dharma talk, followed by group discussion. Fall into bed at ten.

The squeak of a screen door brought me back to the present as a rush of heat displaced the air-conditioned chill. Autumn sunshine spotlighted our facilitator in the doorway. Fair-skinned and blond, he tiptoed around pillows and outstretched legs. His white robes billowed as he made his way to the platform.

Robes?

Without introducing himself, he popped a videocassette into an audiovisual system and dimmed the overhead lights. I assumed it was dramatic flair; surely the *good evening, friends* would come later.

PI Teacher's flickering image materialized on two television monitors. His horn-rimmed glasses framed deep-set black eyes. White hair, ever-present grin, and chubby cheeks gave him an impish appearance. Deep furrows played across his golden skin when he spoke. "Seek happiness only inside yourself, because everything outside changes. Resistance to this truth is madness. Surrender to—"

Thud. A brunette hardly a hairbreadth away from my shawl-wrapped toes plopped onto all fours and waggled her bottom back and forth. She situated herself on a stack of blankets, then rose and tried a chair, and finally folded her legs beneath a bench.

I shifted to get a better view of PI Teacher's face. Two stations east of Lady Waggler, a pony-tailed woman vibrated. Leaning back on her elbows, her legs crossed at the knees, she bounced one shin up and down like a piston.

On the monitor, the videotaped audience leaned in with rapt attention as PI Teacher lectured.

Something sputtered to my left. The noise emanated from a spot where sofa cushions, blankets, and beanbag pillows surrounded an orange-clad matron in a beach chair. The lady I'd bumped heads with. Madame Tracksuit picked up a pillow, threw it onto the floor, tenderized it with her fist, shoved it under her knee, and repeated the violence with the other pillow.

I'd settled into my spot with minimal fuss; I was a pro. The muscles at the base of my neck tightened at the prospect of sitting among these amateurs.

Laugh lines danced around PI Teacher's eyes. His Indian lilt transformed his words into music. "Resistance is madness."

The dharma talk ended two hours later, with the guru bowing low to his audience.

Back in real life, our facilitator flicked on the lights. I waited for the discussion to begin. Instead, he said, "We'll meet again at nine a.m. Take rest." He swept out of the room.

We marched back to our dorm, a long, low building with a single hallway that opened into two-bedroom suites. I opened the door into my suite's closet-sized entry and stopped in the bathroom to wash my face. Strands of long brown hair—not mine—clung to the sides of the sink. As I was debating whether to swear at them or wash them down the drain, a shadow crossed the threshold. I peeked through the door, which was ajar. Lady Waggler. Let her clean up her own hair.

At four o'clock in the morning we trekked from the dorm to the meditation hall for an optional pre-dawn sitting. Cornstalks in a field bordering the pathway witnessed our journey. I'd never walked through a night so black and still. Even the sky was asleep.

The magic wore off inside the hall. Four a.m. was a nice place to visit, but I sure couldn't live there. As soon as my eyes closed, I dozed off.

The involuntary nap didn't help. After breakfast, PI Teacher's disembodied voice emanated from wall-mounted speakers, no video. He instructed us to focus on the sensation of the breath passing over the tip of the nostrils.

I felt the sensation of sleep overtaking me. Again. Drowsiness was interrupted by sounds I hadn't heard since we'd put a new roof on our house. Lady Waggler was dragging her furniture collection to the back row. She destroyed three meditation stations along the way, which set off a chain reaction of reconstruction.

Obviously, she doesn't know how to ignore her discomfort. I attacked my search for peace with renewed resolve, rubbing my tight shoulders.

PI Teacher continued his lesson. "The mind—" Ms. Pony Tail popped her chewing gum.

"—spends most of the time lost in fantasies—"

Wasn't there a Carol Burnett episode about bubble gum?

"—and anticipating the future—"

I'll Google it next week when I get home.

"—never realizing the peace that—"

Geez, did somebody just belch?

While we meditated, PI Teacher chanted prayers of compassion in a relentless monotone.

I prayed he'd stop.

He repeated rote instructions. "Focus on your breathing." "Watch your breath." "Follow the inhale." His accent made it difficult to discern if he'd switched from English to the Buddha's native Pali. I could meditate in peace if only he'd quit … oh … *res*piration. I thought he'd said observe my *des*peration.

The evening videos of his dharma talks compensated for the hard work of each day. Animated gestures and funny sound effects highlighted his storytelling. "It's the law of impermanence, *anicca.*" It sounded like a sneeze. Ah-neé-chah. "Everything you desire and all that you seek to avoid will change." He relayed the dharma like someone reciting his favorite joke, chortling all the way to the punch line. "Seek happiness only inside yourself."

Night after night, the lights came up, and I expected a question-and-answer session. I wanted to ask, Why was PI Teacher laughing? But night after night, our facilitator gathered his robes around him and dumbfounded me with the same two words. "Take rest."

Returning to my room for an afternoon shower, I stifled a screech when a grasshopper flew past my face. A second one sent me leaping into the cornfield. I looked around to make sure no one had seen me. Once in the bathroom, I pulled back the shower curtain. A cricket strolled across a mat of hair in the tub. *Dammit.* I opted to "take rest," but a nap proved out of the question too, because another cricket hopped from a corner of my bedroom and hid under the desk. I had to get out of there. Nature belonged on television, not jumping up all around me.

PI Teacher's recorded voice challenged us to remain motionless for an hour. Finally, the silent retreat was silent.

But during the breaks, Madame Tracksuit (in metallic white) remodeled. By dinnertime, she'd transformed her pile of pillows into a lounge chair, complete with headrest, footstool, and cup holders.

If I could sit still, why couldn't she? Why couldn't any of them? I glared holes in the motionless backs of the zafu-sitters, who reposed in lotus at the front, oblivious to the suffering at the rear. Who had they bribed for their luxury seats in the quiet section?

PI Teacher instructed us to spend two days observing the various itches, twinges, tingles, prickles, and chills that erupted throughout our bodies. The class moved on without me. I was still trying to locate feelings in my nose. "Meditate no matter what you're doing. Do everything with awareness."

Ms. Pony Tail drummed her fingers on the hardwood floor. I gritted my teeth, with awareness.

Lady Waggler's hair accumulated in the tub. I smacked the shower curtain, with awareness.

I fell into bed, exhausted, but couldn't sleep. A cricket was hiding somewhere in my room. I cringed at the chirping, with awareness.

Ms. Pony Tail's zabuton invaded the spot previously occupied by my feet. With my jaw clenched, I nudged her to point out she'd trespassed on pre-owned real estate. She bowed in apology and smiled when she pulled her mat away from my chair.

Her sweet demeanor startled me; I'd expected an exasperated sigh. I glanced away. We were packed in shoulder to shoulder. It was impossible to claim a spot that didn't violate your neighbor's personal space, yet no one's face registered the annoyance that twisted mine into a grimace. I was beginning to feel like Attila the Hun at a peace rally.

Oh. *Those* sensations at the tip of the nostrils. Who would have guessed there was so much going on in the nose?

Sleepiness lifted just long enough for me to taste what I'd been missing. A sweet spot, popping with life: an itch, an air current passed over my cheek, an airplane droned in the distance, a fly buzzed, a mental picture of the dining hall flashed, an opinion emerged from nothingness—evaporated just shy of completing itself. All of it devoid of time. My sweet spot turned sour when somebody started sniffling, every thirty seconds, steady as a metronome. The gloppy breathing made me long for the indifference of sleep. I felt a new sensation: an ache in my shoulders traveling down my back.

A long hot shower would help. With any luck, my roommate might have cleaned the bathroom. No luck. A cricket perched on the mat hanging across the tub. Strands of hair slithered down the side. Without thinking about it, I folded the mat around the cricket, took it outside, and set the critter free. The door to our suite open mid-swing, doorknob still in my grasp, it occurred to me what I'd just done. Or somebody had done it. Lord knows, I'd never gotten that close to a bug. Not on purpose, anyway. It would add a cheery surprise if Lady Waggler cleaned her hair out of the tub.

Seek happiness only inside yourself.

The bathroom mirror reflected a face hardened into a scowl. That was not a happy woman. It made me sad to look at her. I swished Lady Waggler's hair down the drain with a blast of water from the showerhead, then stepped into the stream and blasted the tension from my lower back.

A hubbub after dinner delayed the start of the evening session. Retreat staff signaled to each other. They counted the cushion piles, tried the bathroom door. One of them left the hall.

Geez. Now what?

She returned with Lady Waggler, who lumbered to her spot. She winced when she curled onto her chair. Her face contorted.

That sound, that look. I'd groaned like that for weeks after spraining a knee. I remembered the searing pain that had sliced through my injured joint. *This poor woman hurts.*

"How you doin'?" Madame Tracksuit approached on the pathway, adorned in iridescent lavender. Her close-cropped hair looked painted on, with c-shaped spit curls in front of her ears. "This is intense, and I have a feeling it's going to get worse."

Why's she talking to me at a silent retreat?

"My daughter got me into this," she said.

"You ever meditate before?"

"No. If you hear somebody screaming, that's me."

I chuckled in sympathy. "Thanks for the warning."

She was learning meditation by doing it ten hours straight for ten days in a row. Without the support of a flesh-and-blood teacher to offer a "good work, you're on the right track." My resolve paled next to hers. She sped off, and I shout-whispered after her, "Good luck."

One day remained before we broke the silence. Surely our mute facilitator would offer instructions. I plodded to the meditation hall, anticipating the sound of a voice other than PI Teacher's. A sign hung on the door. *Silence will end at 9 a.m. tomorrow.* It provided no details, merely dangled the hope of a commuted sentence.

After breakfast the following day, Madame Tracksuit (in glow-in-the-dark pink) caught up with me again. "New instructions for today," she said. "We can talk pretty soon."

I patted her on the shoulder. "You must be pretty happy."

She nodded. "But it's been good. It's good to get quiet." She scurried away.

At nine a.m., the atmosphere in the meditation hall was coiled in anticipation, although the facilitator relaxed in royal ease on his zabuton. He leaned forward, certainly about to congratulate the group on a great retreat. Wrong. Without so much as a glance in our direction, he turned off the sound, monitors, lights, and air conditioning. Straightened his robes around him and tiptoed out of the house. I didn't know what to do. Everyone else seemed confused too; the room was more quiet than it had been in the past ten days.

Madame Tracksuit leaped to her feet. "Thank you, Jesus! It's over."

The hall erupted in chaos. Newbies in the back squealed, chattered, and giggled, while stoic veterans in front greeted each other with namasté. Mass hugging erased the aisle that previously separated damsels from dudes. The mob spilled out into the parking lot like a flock of geese descending on a pond. I was stunned, used to the hushed tones of a formal closing circle, in which we reflected on how we'd experienced the week, what insights we'd gained about ourselves. But this ... the noise was too intense, the change too abrupt. I felt assaulted.

A woman wrapped in a shawl escaped to a bench away from the crowd, an empty seat beside her. I inched closer. "Is this taken?"

"No. Sorry, I'm not very talkative. This part's always too jarring for me."

"Always? You've done this retreat before?"

"Three times."

"What do you get from it?"

"I keep seeing how crazy my mind is. Can't believe it's in charge of my life."

At lunchtime, I trudged to the dining hall. I must have misread the schedule. I must have miscounted the days. A sign posted next to the double door ordered us back into the silence for the following morning.

Another day? Back into the silence? No.

I pushed on the door. It stuck. I pushed with my shoulder. Nothing. Leaned into it. It didn't budge. Madame Tracksuit, in fire engine red, came up from behind, hugged me, and breezed through the unlocked side. The door slapped shut behind her.

Laugh lines danced around PI Teacher's eyes. "Resistance is madness."

Well, why didn't you tell me that ten days ago?

I followed Madame Tracksuit into the noisy dining hall. "I'm Georgia," she said. "My daughter took this course last year. She was so calm afterward. She paid for me to take it, too. Thought it would help my tension headaches." By the end of dinner, I'd met them all. Lady Waggler—Patricia—had strained her back right before the retreat but wanted to come anyway. Ms. Pony Tail—

Linda—was just out of college, but she'd already taken the course twice before.

As I walked to the last meditation sitting, a grasshopper landed square on my chest, head pointed at mine. I stopped. It seemed the most natural thing in the world to peer into his bulging eyes, as though I chatted with grasshoppers on a regular basis. The world shrank down to the two of us, neither one twitching, no destination other than this patch of dirt, until he hopped into the cornfield.

During PI Teacher's recorded closing lecture, my neighbors vibrated, twitched, squirmed, coughed, muttered, sneezed, and belched. Linda popped her gum. Georgia pounded her pillows. Patricia rubbed her aching back. My breath eased, silky, across the tip of my nose. *Take rest.*

HOLDING ON, LETTING GO

I

Gardens of Delight Studio. I positioned a blue yoga mat so the long sides lined up precisely with the seams in the hardwood floor, and the short sides crossed the seams at a ninety-degree angle. I unfurled a green mat atop the blue one. The green was a hand-width too short, so a strip of blue protruded from underneath, like the yoga mat's slip was showing. I'd experimented with other combinations, hoping to avoid this unsightly length differential. I had tried the pink ones and even the pretty purple one, but this proved the only pair that worked properly, for three reasons: 1) The chemistry of the green mat kept my hands from slipping; 2) The combined thickness protected my knees from the floor; 3) The colors matched my underwear.

Our teacher, Lynn, set a CD player on the floor beside a vase of lilies, their fragrance filling the room. She plucked a ladybug from a bloom, setting it free out an open window. Every spring ladybugs flew in through the unscreened windows and gathered in clumps where the walls met the ceiling. The second-story studio looked out over the topmost branches of a hackberry tree in Lynn's front yard, as though we were in a tree house. We were serenaded by what I'd assumed was a cardinal, until one of the outdoor-lovers in class had pointed out it was a mockingbird. Nature's bait-and-switch annoyed me. If it sounds like a cardinal, it ought to be a cardinal.

A classmate rolled out her mat next to the wall. "Contractor called me 'young lady' yesterday. Made me so mad."

Another set up beneath the skylight. "I hate it, too. I've earned these years."

Her pile of props ended up too close to mine.

I repositioned three planks away.

A ladybug had landed on my mat. I flicked it away with a click when my fingernail tapped against the shell. Polka-dotted wings unfolded as the ladybug shook off the indignity and wobbled across the floor in a huff. She'd have to find her own spot. No invaders allowed. This was my dominion—a green rectangle of real estate, over which I'd reign with iron fist.

Lynn said, "I missed you guys. Let's shake off the world and do some yoga."

I sat cross-legged, hands in prayer position, as her opening *om* floated over the class. We joined in, half a beat after she began. Sound waves led our voices until they lined up parallel with Lynn's, our pitches matching. By the final *om* we were one voice, strong and confident, holding the *mmm* until our breath gave out.

Lynn pushed a button on the CD player, freeing the soft melody of a flute. Just as I knew she would, just as she did every class, she said, "Come to hands and knees."

I was already in place before she got the words out.

So was the ladybug—planted right between my hands.

II

Sunshine Studio. A substitute teacher sat in Nancy's spot at the check-in counter. When I picked up the pen to sign in, Substitute Teacher did not trill, as Nancy did every Saturday, "Oh honey, you're already signed in. Got you as soon as you walked in the door." Therefore I could not respond, as I did every Saturday, "I love the service in this joint."

ST took her spot at the front of the class. "We'll begin with three *oms*."

My voice landed on Nancy's pitch, instead of ST's, and then wandered around out of tune. But as the unfamiliar teacher led us through familiar poses, muscle memory took over. Standing Forward Bend, which had become my favorite, the way it released the overnight crimp in my lower back. Low Lunge that scissored my legs into flexibility. Downward Facing Dog that made me grin at the upside-down view between my knees.

The class sped up. The names ran together, and by the time I comprehended "left foot forward," ST had moved on to "right foot over your shoulder." She ordered poses when I least anticipated them. My Tree wobbled. My Eagle crashed. My Boat capsized. She didn't give me enough time to find my balance, that fulcrum between holding on and letting go.

And then we were sitting and rocking the baby: yoga-speak for breaking the hip. ST encouraged us toward *astavakrasana*—what the hell was that? I wanted to asta her vakrasana.

I collapsed into Child's Pose to recover.

In child's pose, you prostrate yourself, forehead pressed to the floor, knees bent. Your back is exposed; it senses what's behind you.

What I sensed was my father.

He was at the kitchen table, glaring at my high school report card, which was lying beside the salt shaker.

"You're failing," he said.

At the sink, I shoved a skillet into sudsy water. "Not failing. They're Cs, not Fs."

I gripped the skillet as tightly as I should have held onto those words. How was I to know he'd redrawn the boundaries? How was I to know C meant F? That average meant fail?

He tapped the salt shaker with his fingertip, the rest of him calm as death.

Tap.

"Watch your mouth."

Tap.

His chair scraped away from the table.

Tap.

The kitchen held its breath.

He got to his feet in slow motion, his head just inches from the ceiling. One of his size twelves pointed at me and the other at the doorway. He picked up the salt shaker, set it carefully on top of my report card, and then stalked out of the room.

My neck was hot where his yellow eyes had singed twin holes. As I set the skillet in the drainer, my hand trembled, my movements foreshortened to fit within the confines of Dad's shifting rules.

In child's pose, you prostrate yourself, forehead pressed to the floor, knees bent. Your back is vulnerable, but your arms are extended, and your fingertips reach beyond the boundaries of your mat, farther than you thought possible.

ST said, "Sitting position, legs extended."

I swung around to face her. She hadn't walked among us the way Nancy did, asking how's your wonky knee today. She wouldn't notice my mat askew on the floor, and how I let it lie there crooked, outside the boundaries I'd imposed just minutes before.

III

Gardens of Delight Studio. Lynn paced in front of our mats. "Pair up for partner work."

Theoretically, partners pulled, tugged, leaned on, and pushed against each other to encourage a wider range of motion than either could summon individually.

Invariably, partners pulled an inappropriate body part, tugged in an unexpected direction, leaned at a dangerous incline, and pushed too hard. Their knees bent at a different angle than mine. They scooted my mats out of place.

Lynn paired us up. "Marilyn and Dawn. One sit, the other stand behind."

I sat cross-legged, hands clasped behind my head. Standing behind me, Marilyn bent forward over my head, wove her straight arms between my bent ones like a lattice pie crust, and placed her palms between my scapulas. Lynn's voice guided me into territory painful to my age-tightened joints. "Lean into the support of your partner."

I tilted backward and pushed against Marilyn. Her palms pressed against my upper back, the spot where a mother's hand holds a baby to her shoulder. She stood firm, her legs braced and her arms shaped into a buttress that forced my shoulders back and my chest up, a shape outside the pre-drawn lines of my established pattern.

In this pose, your ribcage expands. It exposes your heart, which takes in the world around you.

What I took in was Dad and Mama.

They were arguing behind their closed bedroom door.

I crept out of bed, our house too hot with anger for sleep. I couldn't breathe, nor make sense of the words—his voice thundering, hers pitched high—but I flinched, my arms protecting my head, in case the words were aimed at me.

Curl up in a ball, get tiny, disappear. Don't you dare be discovered crouched on the stair if that door cracks open.

Lynn walked from one mat to another to another. "Trust your partner. She's got you. Let go."

The weak muscles in my lower back struggled to keep me vertical, but their effort only intensified a cramp in my stiff neck, until a sharp pain stabbed the base of my skull. Sustain this iron grip a second longer, I would break. Relax, I would fall. Down, down. Break my crown. Tumble into my childhood.

I groaned, sipped a breath, and blowing out, surrendered backward into Marilyn's palms. Her arms and hands caught my full weight. My breastbone jutted forward awkwardly. New blood, filled with oxygen, rushed into tissues previously hardened by habit. The torrent over-topped well-worn grooves and burst through knots, which exploded into inconsequential fragments. The pain dissolved.

"Okay," Lynn said. "Switch places. Return the favor."

I wriggled free. I wanted to thank Marilyn, but words caught in my throat.

Memories sound like feather-light things. They should float away on a dust mote. But it took the strength in Marilyn's hands to lift an old story from my shoulders. How could I return such a favor?

IV

Sunshine Studio. I positioned my mat perpendicular to Nancy's. The corners touched and the short front edges formed a right angle. On the floor in front of us, a candle burned inside a globe. Other than that, the studio was lit by only a string of miniature white Christmas lights.

Nancy had created a sunrise class for the holiday season. "Troubled times," she'd said when she'd introduced the idea. "Let's spend December sending peace into the world."

I peeled off my sweater and tossed it onto the floor. "Where's everybody?"

"Looks like just you and me today."

She led me through poses to ease the stiffness from my muscles. We chanted *Shanti shanti shanti* to coax peace into our hearts. We bowed, so close I felt the air disturbed around our heads, like overlapping ripples in a pond.

"We'll sit for a while." Her cue to begin meditation.

Concentrate. *Shanti.* Why does a peace sign look the same as V for victory? *Shanti.* I'm cold … I should have kept my sweater on … *Shanti.* Did I turn off my phone? … Darn it. *Shanti* … I, I, I … Everything's about me … Why can't I …?

I focused on the space around the word *shanti.* I released the word *sweater.*

Thoughts petered out.

From torrent to trickle.

The final trickle absorbed into the pre-dawn quiet of the studio.

The candle flickered light into amorphous patterns.

Beneath my skin, atoms swarmed like microscopic bees. In their wake, the winter chill dissipated.

I released *winter.*

My viewpoint floated away from its perch behind my eyes, riding thermals of consciousness until I was looking down from the ceiling, at the top of my head, Nancy's too, our bent knees touching. We were still as lotus blossoms. The image faded. Viewpoint materialized across the room, from where we were shadowed figures sitting cross-legged. I could see Nancy's side, her face in profile. From this angle, we were conjoined at our shoulders. Twin Buddhas in a candle-lit temple. Buddhas receded, as if into a fog. Mist lifted; my face was in close-up, the pores on my nose tip transformed into pixels in an image. Yet Nancy remained in the frame. From every vantage point, our figures overlapped in a single shape-shifting curve. A nancydawn.

I released *peace*.

"Very gently, open your eyes."

When I did, viewpoint settled on its roost behind my lids.

Nancy was smiling. She looked mischievous, like she'd just performed a magic trick.

"Is it chilly in here?" she asked.

A draft brushed the back of my neck.

Ought to buy a long-sleeved yoga top. No, too expensive. Find a sale. Is there time to …?

I picked up my sweater. "Now that you mention it, it is cold." But I let the sweater fall from my hand.

Shanti. Shanti. Shanti.

CHURCH WORK

I stood when my name was read from the guest book at Second Baptist Church. Worshipers twisted around in their pews to get a good look. Having visited other churches, I knew this routine. Behind anonymous smiles, they were appraising the relative demureness of my attire and rating the level of Christian piety in my demeanor. I refused to give them the satisfaction of seeing me squirm.

I met the gazes of those who'd turned to look, giving them a queenly nod.

After all visitors had been introduced, Pastor Howard spread his arms, the full sleeves of his white robe like angels' wings. "Won't you please remain standing and allow us to give you a proper Second Baptist welcome?" He paused. "Okay, church, let's go to work."

A wailing chord exploded from the organ. Windows rattled. Floorboards shook. A wave of chatter rumbled over the pews; hellos bounced off the walls. Laughter rose to the ceiling and rained down on my head. The congregation surged into the aisles and bore down on me, a sanctified tornado with arms poking out like telephone poles torn from the ground. Before I could duck, the arms consumed me. "Welcome." "Nice to have you here." "Welcome." "Morning." "Bless you."

I could only stammer. "Thank you. Thank you."

The next time I went to Second Baptist, the guest book lay open on the welcome table, every blank line a puzzle. How many visits before you were no longer a visitor? I signed in, but felt a little guilty when my name was announced. Pastor Howard smiled as usual. "We're happy to have you with us again this morning." He moved on to quiz the other guests, *Where are you from? How did you find us? Do you have a church home?* Then he spread his arms. "Okay, church, let's go to work."

Windows rattled. The floor shook. The organist pounded the keyboard—he'd added a drummer for reinforcements. I was less of a novelty than the first time; there were breaks in the hand-shaking. I eavesdropped. Behind me, two ladies hadn't seen one another since one of them had hip surgery. Another pair hadn't met since Mother Jones' funeral.

Sundays marched by, and the landscape took on a familiar shape. The third pew from the front had extra legroom. It was reserved for a clutch of bent-over matrons who parked wheel-chairs and walkers. Behind the disabled parking sat Sister Pearl, who frequently strode in late. She always paused to greet me, kiss-ing the air beside my cheek and leaving a scent of citrusy perfume in her wake. Her pew filled in with a white-haired couple and their great-grandson and a woman who ran the Thursday night marriage class. I sat behind Sister Pearl.

"Church, let's go to work."

The organist got a head start on the chatter explosion, and he'd called in a trumpeter to supplement the drummer, but they still lost the battle for decibels. I had stopped signing the guest book, which ended my right to the official welcome. I remained seated in content obscurity, until a woman leaned out of the tor-nado and reached for my hand. "Good morning, how are you?" I opened my mouth to answer, but she was washed downstream. Here came another. "Good to see you." And another.

Me? Why?

"Okay, church, let's go to work."

Was I now part of the church that must go to work? Should I join in or stay out of the way? An ace bandage around my knee gave me cover. I feigned temporary disability. Pretended to read the hymnal, then pretended to search through my purse for tissues. But no one asked why I wasn't performing my churchly responsibilities. No one glanced at me with suspicion. How long could I justify my ambivalence? After all, a visitor is a person who needs to ask directions to the restroom. By this time, I knew three different routes.

Another week went by. The guest list was short, only one name. A young woman who looked as though a gust would blow her over.

That was me, the first day I had stood as a visitor. Then the Second Baptist welcome had rolled over me. One by one, those Baptists had taken my hand, and each encounter was the calm in the middle of the storm. It was fitting to pass the welcome along to a solitary young woman.

I could do that. Say hello. Turn around. Return to my pew. This greeting thing was fraught with peril. It could be a surreptitious test for those who inhabited the limbo between guest and member of the family. I waited to shake the young woman's hand and turned to reclaim my seat. The crowd was going in the opposite direction. I squeezed through sideways. Bumped shoulders. "Excuse me." Stepped on toes. "Sorry." I listened for muttered criticism but heard only cheery voices.

After I got back to my spot, nervous energy kept me on my feet. A soprano who'd tut-tutted my bandaged leg the week before was marching toward the visitor. She stopped beside me, waggling a finger. "Should you be standing? How's your knee?" A deaconess descended from the platform and waved as she approached. She would point out my *faux pas*. Disapproval would be dripping from her voice. She rested her hands on my shoulders. "I've so enjoyed seeing you smiling out here every week. I hope you'll be coming back."

"Okay, church. Let's go to work."

Windows rattled. The floor shook.

I let the tornado suck me into the aisle. I surged toward a family who had just been introduced. "Welcome. Nice to have you here." The crowd swept me toward the sanctuary doors, across the back row where the ushers sat, and down the aisle on the other side.

Brother Organist shook my hand without missing a note. "Morning, Miss Dawn." A woman sitting beside her walker reached up to hug me. "Hello, sugar."

Momentum was slowing as I reached Sister Pearl. She took my hand in hers and kissed the air beside my cheek. It was an offering, granted Sunday after Sunday, without fail. I breathed in the scent of her perfume, citrus, not too sweet.

The tornado petered out and dropped me on the very spot it had lifted me from. The pew behind Sister Pearl. My seat.

SEDUCED

I was standing by myself in the center of the crowded room.

Stiff as rigor mortis.

This did not happen. Not here.

Excited about attending a Kirtan for the first time, I crossed a parking lot from my air-conditioned car into an air-conditioned yoga studio. The glass door snugged closed, freeing me from triple-digit heat. I paused to thank every Hindu deity I could imagine for relief from summer's oppression.

Tucking my shoes into a cubbyhole—a welcome bit of yoga familiarity in a studio that was otherwise new to me—I grabbed a song sheet from a stack on a table and then slipped into the main room. It was filled with folding chairs. I claimed a seat in the front row. A few young women had already unfurled yoga mats and were sitting cross-legged on the floor in front of the chairs. Others sprawled on cushions.

Beneath miniature white lights strung in lazy loops across the ceiling, musicians were transforming one corner into a stage, arranging amplifiers, microphones, cords, and instruments. Instruments that Darren, the guitarist, would later introduce like visiting dignitaries. *Mridanga*, a floor drum of southern India. *Tablas*, hand drums from the north by way of ancient Arabia. Harmonium, a keyboard originally from England.

Fay, the lead singer, played the harmonium. She directed us to a chant at the bottom of our song sheets. A call and response, Fay sang the call and Darren led the audience response. "*Hare Krishna. Hare Krishna. Krishna Krishna. Hare Hare.*" My voice at first uncertain. I grew more confident with every verse. "*Hare Rama. Hare Rama. Rama Rama. Hare Hare.*" Punctuated by the heartbeat of tablas, the chant captivated me, with a promise of ascension—from the chair ... from the earth.

The studio filled; our sparse numbers multiplied into a crowd. As a group slipped into the row behind me, their cotton shirts brushed the back of my neck. I remained the only person in my row ... the only African-American in the room. I suspected a connection but turned away from suspicion toward the promise of ascension.

Darren leaned into his mic. "If you're new to Kirtan, don't worry. Join in. Dance if the music moves you. Soak up the energy."

I glanced at the typewritten page on my lap, lifted my voice in adoration, and soaked up the energy.

After exalting Lord Krishna, we called on the goddesses. Fay's soprano shimmered. The divine feminine beckoned. We followed. We appealed to the goddess of art and creativity. "*He Saraswati.*" The goddess of prosperity and wealth. "*He Maha Lakshmi.*" The goddess of transformation and death. "*He Mata Kali.*" I came to them like a child. "*Jagatambe Jai Jai Ma. Jagatambe Jai Jai Ma.*" They smothered me with kisses.

Incense sweetened the air. Fingers of smoke drifted in ever-shifting directions as latecomers trickled in. A man and woman grabbed chairs at the opposite end of my row and scooted them farther away, as if positioning for a better view, even though the people in front were on the floor. Sitting at one end of a long empty row, I felt like a single person on a teeter-totter.

Sanskrit made me tongue-tied, but the next chant began slowly enough for me to pick up pronunciations. *Om* terra. *Too*-terra. Too-*ray*. So-*hah*. Syllables popped from my throat—I was the drum. "*Om* terra. *Too*-terra." I rocked from side to side. "Too-*ray*. So-*hah*." The chant sped up. "*Om* terra. *Too*-terra. Too-*ray*. So-*hah*." Rhythm captured my feet. "*Om* terra. *Too*-terra. Too-*ray*. So-*hah*." I welcomed oblivion. Shatter me. Blast the shards to the winds. I wasn't singing any longer, only sputtering guttural noises, desperate for Tara to take me, my voice giving out for lack of breath, and as the percussionist pounded a final thunderclap, Darren swung his guitar over his head and mimed smashing it onto the stage. Praise God!

Fay rose from her seat at the harmonium and knelt on the floor, crystal bowls lined up at her knees. She smiled demurely. "We'll slow the energy down a bit, so you can drive home safely." She swiped a wooden stick around the rims of the bowls and began the closing chant. I was disappointed the lyrics were in English, which normally triggered my intellect to spring into analysis and debate. By this point in the evening, though, my mind had surrendered. After rounds of "Peace across the land and in the deep blue sea," a longing for peace trickled down my cheeks in rivulets. My voice shook. I could only mouth the final words. A deep tone from the largest crystal bowl lingered … faded … faded …

The musicians bowed to us. I lowered my head. "Namaste."

Eyes closed, I waited for my emotions to settle and for the rustle of an audience preparing to leave. But instead of *goodnight, thank you for coming*, Fay announced, "We're going to end with a ritual to honor the light in each of us. Choose a partner and stand facing each other."

Still in a fog, I rose from my chair. Waves of motion rippled across the room, as chairs and cushions were pushed aside. There was a milling around, the chatter of voices, the slip and pad of bare feet. Pairs sprouted along the walls and in the corners. Twos grew into fours and then sixes, which eddied around the studio, filling in the empty spaces. The figures were ghostly, floating in incense clouds and the half-light of a setting sun. When the mingling slowed to a standstill, and the chatter faded to murmur, and the choosing was complete—

I was alone in the center of the room.

Stiff as rigor mortis.

This did not happen.

Not here.

Of course it happened.

Here.

I should have seen it coming.

Stupid, stupid woman. To be seduced by the possibility of love in a room full of white people was as reckless as mooning over a married man.

I wanted to run, but fleeing would only draw attention. The only thing that would save me from humiliation was the invisibility that had caused it. That, and hatred. My eyes narrowed to slits, my cheeks flushed hot, I coiled, ready to savage this roomful of devotees. My fists gnarled into witch's hands with hooked nails to tear bloody stripes across the backs these worshipers had turned on me, to rip all those pink feet from their shocked ankles—feet that walked away from me and danced to the beat of God's lying heart.

A command from the stage startled my hatred. "You two pair up."

Fay was spotlighted under the twinkling lights, one hand pointed at a lone woman on the far side of the studio, the other at me. The woman hurried toward me. Malice retreated down into my gut, letting my eye slits open in welcome.

Just get through it, Dawn.

Nose to nose with our partners, we formed two concentric circles. Those on the inside faced out, those on the outside faced in. Music swelled; we sang a verse; the outer circle shifted to the right. I was opposite a different partner. We chanted and bowed. Singing into those other eyes, I was looking into faces of innocence, moonlit orbs that reflected *namasté*. When the light in me bowed to the light in each of my partners, my personality, with its crown of slights, dissolved. We were unspoiled. We were pure of motive, every one of us.

Soon enough the exercise ended. Regulars exploded out of their reverie into chatty groups, and still I expected someone to offer an outstretched hand in welcome. None did.

I threaded through knots of well-wishers to compliment the musicians. Darren was stuffing cords into a plastic bin. I hoped he hadn't noticed me un-chosen in the middle of the room, and also hoped he had. We hugged and laughed, my *hello, that was wonderful* followed by his *so glad you were here, thanks for coming*. His effervescence seemed an indication he had not noticed. My good cheer, on the other hand, was a nervous habit. Our words swallowed by the surrounding din, I turned away, intending to say hello to Fay. I hoped for a remorseful acknowledgement of the scene she'd witnessed, which would rewind the last hour back to the promise of *"Hare Krishna. Krishna. Krishna."* But she was chatting with an acquaintance.

My feet stuck to the floor. Go? Stay? I was rickety, nailed together with mismatched emotions.

Joyful.

Betrayed.

Uplifted.

Sublime.

Ashamed.

Cherished.

Abandoned.

When I opened the door to leave the studio, the summer night seared my face—heat so oppressive it was hard to breathe.

BAH HUMBUG

I'd lost the spirit of Christmas in a frenzied dash through the snow past blow-up Santas, oceans of poinsettias, and sleighs that dangled from traffic lights, from Macy's to HyVee to the liquor store to the jewelry store to Lowe's (with a brief stop at church on the Sunday before the big day)—all to the tune of Salvation Army bell-ringing. I binged on green-sprinkled star-shaped cookies and outgrew my sexy New Year's Eve outfit long before the occasion to wear it. I abandoned a cart full of gifts in a crowded department store aisle, having grown too tired to remain upright in a forty-minute checkout line. I strung lights around every window in my house, changed the sheets to red flannel, swagged the mantel, dragged the tree from the basement, and topped it with a star long after my bedtime. Come January I couldn't face the chore of un-decorating: the tree twinkled in my living room until Valentine's Day. That was the final blow. With no children at home, I resigned from Christmas.

Every winter, I lived in a parallel universe, calm and smug alongside the holiday madness, cynical about everyone else's holiday motives … until the year my office co-workers voted to have a Secret Santa gift exchange. It was majority rule, everybody in or everybody out. In our workplace of sixty, the final tally was fifty-nine to one.

I would cooperate, but I would not be happy.

To begin our anonymous gift exchange, we each wrote a Christmas list and tossed it into a hat. I drew the data analyst whose office was next to mine. I'll call her Noelle, because every year, just after Memorial Day, her computer, phone, guest chair, and bulletin board began wearing Santa hats.

On her Secret Santa list, Noelle had recorded a taste for unique recipes and a penchant for collecting frogs.

Frogs?

I'd heard of spoon collections. But frogs?

The day I pulled Noelle's name from the hat, I stopped after work at a drug store to buy aspirin. From the bottom shelf of a case populated with stuffed animals, a lime green frog looked up at me. It had a lopsided smile, spindly legs, and pancake-sized feet. I picked it up to examine the price tag. My goodness, he was as soft as my favorite fleece hoodie and as warm as my flannel sheets. Before I could stop myself, I held him against my cheek. Lime Green Froggie and I left the store together.

I slipped the gift into Noelle's office while she attended a meeting. After she returned, I peeked in. Froggie sat on her computer monitor, long legs and big feet dangling in front of the screen. I walked in, and she picked him up as though he were her first grandbaby. "Look what my Secret Santa got me. I love him. Feel how soft he is."

She held him close to her heart. Tears welled in her eyes.

I felt warm and fuzzy. A lot like Froggie.

I was elbowing my way through Target. At the end of the auto supplies aisle, another stuffed frog. A button on this one's stomach read, "Push here." I obliged. The frog croaked to the tune of Jingle Bells. "Ribbit-ribbit-ribbit. Ribbit-ribbit-ribbit. Ribbit-ribbit-ribbit-ribbit-ribbit."

Noelle had a reputation for practical jokes. This was the frog for her.

I lay in wait until the lunch hour left our suite deserted. Like a cat burglar, I cracked open her office door, snuck in, and set the frog on her chair. Once in my own office, I paced and strained to hear a reaction. At last, an ear-splitting cackle resounded through the hallway. Noelle burst through my door, armed with the frog. "You gotta see this." She pushed the button. The frog croaked. I laughed, but only politely, not wanting to give myself away. But bursting from the desire to claim credit as a genius gift-giver.

According to the rumor mill, for the next six days the frog broke into song during finance meetings, strategic planning sessions, and teambuilding discussions. Noelle's chortle echoed through the halls.

I rounded the corner toward my office. She'd cornered the finance director outside my office door. "Did I show you this?"

"Yes. Twice."

Noelle had already pushed the button. "I can't wait to find out who my Secret Santa is."

The victim narrowed her eyes. "Neither can I."

I slipped through my door, wearing my best innocent bystander expression.

Frogs invaded my dreams. They appeared in cloud formations. My favorite nature show ran a four-part series on the reproductive cycle of the Vietnamese Mossy Frog. There were more croakers in my life than there were in Noelle's.

Determined to liberate myself, I focused the last gift on her love of cooking. I embarked on a cyber treasure hunt, searching the Internet for exotic recipes. I printed them on Christmas tree-green paper, rolled them up into a scroll, and tied them with green and white satin ribbon. The final touch was a gift card picturing a frog wearing a Santa hat.

She and an accounts payable clerk walked into her office after grabbing morning coffee from the break room. "My Secret Santa's been here. I hope it's recipes." For the rest of the day, whenever I ran into her, I overheard her in the hallways, over coffee, and on the phone, describing her plans to try out her new recipes.

I was as proud as a five-year-old seeing my newest drawing displayed on the family fridge.

We revealed our identities at our office Christmas party. Evergreen swags were draped across the tables, their fragrance filling the room. A CD played in the background. *Jingle Bells* faded into *Little Drummer Boy* into *Chestnuts Roasting on an Open Fire* into *We Three Kings*. The chatter of overlapping conversations floated over the music. Holiday excitement was at its peak; for most of us, it was the last day of work before Christmas.

On discovering I was her benefactor, Noelle wrapped me in a bosomy embrace, the kind of hug you save for a long-absent friend. I held her for half a beat longer than she held me.

We filled our plates and sat side by side. I crunched on a reindeer cookie, while she described the frogs at her house—painted on the mailbox, embroidered on bedroom slippers, and hopping across toilet seat covers. The noise threatened to swallow her voice, so I scooted in till our heads were touching. I didn't want to miss a single frog.

HOW TO SURVIVE CHRISTMAS ALONE

December 17.

Pull the covers over your head to block the morning light, and rest in the spot where your husband ought to be.

Remember lazing here in bed beside him, propped up with pillows, a map spread between you. You had traced the highways and picked the overnight towns between home and the retreat center out east, where you had planned to spend the last two weeks of the year. It turned out you wanted to stay home. It also turned out Ben still wanted to go. Ordinarily your disagreements ended with one of you saying *I don't feel strongly. Let's do what you want.* This one had ended with him standing quietly in his truth and you standing quietly in yours. Remember how your certainty had caught you off guard?

Wince at the prize you've won by standing in your truth: Christmas Alone. Your family spread across the country and you without a plane ticket, your friends with families of their own and you without an invitation.

Think about being one with what-is.

Think about surrendering to each moment.

Think how un-enlightened you are. You don't want to be one with Christmas Alone.

Suspect if you were a better person—generous, kind, considerate—invitations would flood your email and your voice mail.

Get out of bed and check your voice mail. Feel ridiculous.

Eat breakfast. Write. Eat lunch. Write. Eat dinner.

Drive to yoga class.

On your way home, curse the shortened winter days. Curse the dark driveway. Curse the gloomy house. Fumble with the remote control. The garage door groans open. Hesitate as the car idles. Idle with the car. Once inside the garage, pause before pushing the button to close the door behind you. Before crossing the threshold into the house, stop again, one hand on the doorknob.

December 18.

An out-of-town friend calls. Recognize her country-singer drawl and calculate: she lives by herself four hours away; you could visit her, stay overnight, return on the twenty-sixth, the whole Christmas Alone problem solved.

A country-singer drawl cuts through your calculations. Your friend is worried her forgetfulness is turning into Alzheimer's. She's panicked she'll be trapped inside her mind, inside a nightmare.

Remember your grandmother. Fighting with the lock on the front door. She'd tugged the handle, and the deadbolt had banged against the door jamb. Her bony fingers had stuck out from the sleeves of a jogging suit, and the pants were falling off her skinny bottom.

"Where you going?" you'd asked.

"Home," she'd said.

"You *are* home."

A country-singer drawl cuts through your memories. You should console your friend, but instead think at least you're not afraid of Alzheimer's. Feel un-enlightened.

December 19.

Make a joyful noise at Second Baptist Church. "Hark the herald angels sing, glory to the newborn king." Pat your feet. Sing off-key. Feel both anonymous and essential.

Twin girls read the announcements in high-pitched pubescent

voices. The church is providing dinner for anyone who's Alone On Christmas. Laugh when the pastor interrupts the twins, "Don't get between me and the sweet potato pie."

Remember sweet potato pie, cinnamon, and clove on your tongue.

Imagine little boys in grown-up suits and red bow ties. Imagine old women clucking at you to "fill up your plate, child, you ain't bigger than a minute."

Jot down *3:00 Xmas dinner* on the back of the worship program and stick it in your purse.

Hum to yourself all the way down the church steps and across the parking lot, waving goodbye, God bless.

Remember your house. It lies in wait, slack-jawed, ready to suck you into its belly.

Drive to Target. Pretend you don't see the Salvation Army bell ringer. Push a squeaky cart toward cosmetics while Bing Crosby drones on about a white Christmas. Pick up a bottle of lotion. Set it back on the shelf. Pluck a cardigan from the sweater rack. Return it to the rack. Inspect a pair of headphones in electronics. Set them back on the shelf. Jimmy Stewart plays on the big screen televisions. Half a dozen Jimmy Stewarts handing out cash to the bank customers. You're annoyed. Buy dental floss.

At home, discover eBay. Bid on a coat you'd tried on at a department store but were too cheap to buy. Search the Internet for yoga tights. Search for luggage. Feel the life force leech out through your fingertips. Search for headphones.

Slam the laptop shut.

Scream, "What are you doing?"

Try to recall the rhythms of your weekly routine. Check your calendar for last Sunday. Nothing's listed, because Sundays are free days. You don't feel free.

See your grandmother fighting the front door.

December 20.

Stick a note on your laptop: no Internet shopping today.

Eat breakfast. Check your eBay bid.

Pick up *War and Peace* where you left off last month. You don't recognize the characters. You can't tell whether they're at peace or at war.

Meditate.

Fall asleep.

Read.

Fall asleep.

Go to bed at seven o'clock.

Don't fall asleep.

You have no reason to sleep, read, or meditate.

You have no reason not to.

Hop out of bed at eight o'clock. Run the dishwasher. Mop the kitchen floor. Write a check for the water bill. Lay the pen gently on the counter. Whisper, "What are you doing?"

December 21.

At two a.m. throw a down coat over your pajamas and venture onto the patio to witness the eclipse of a blood moon on Winter Solstice. An icy breeze bites your ankles as patchy clouds drift across the heavens. The clouds part and then close. Part and close. Dissipate and reassemble. Each time, the moon re-emerges as an ever-thinner crescent, until the final sliver disappears.

Witness yourself on the patio, in the middle of the night, alone, and calm. Feel yourself dissipate and reassemble.

Go back to bed. Get up again at seven o'clock. Decide to do something fun today. Try to remember fun. Draw a blank.

Check your eBay bid. Search online for yoga tights. Search for luggage. Search for headphones. Read celebrity gossip.

December 22.

Attend your Wednesday night book group. They're surprised to see you. Your Catholic friend says, "Thought you were on retreat with Ben." Remember how welcome you feel at her place. Ask what time she's having Christmas dinner. Paste a fake *that's great* expression on your face when she says, "I'm not. I'm going to my sister-in-law's." Feel like a cage door has slammed shut behind you.

Call your out-of-town friend; anticipate her country-singer drawl.

She's four hours away and at the same time right there in the palm of your hand.

She tells you her girlfriends are all going away for the holidays this year. You laugh ironically at how the universe is handing both of you Christmas Alone. Say, "If the weather's okay, I'll come down." Fail to appreciate the irony when she says, "I won't be here. I'm driving to Little Rock tomorrow."

December 23.

Check your eBay bid. You win. The coat is yours. Feel triumphant. Feel let down.

Insist on fitting entertainment into your day. Write a To-Do list: art museum, grocery store, bank, drugstore. You hate all that running around. Scribble out *art museum*.

Check the forecast. The weatherman is wearing a Santa hat. He says snow all night tonight and all day tomorrow. He looks proud of himself. Curse the weatherman. Curse his Santa hat. Dig the worship program out of your purse, with its *3:00 Xmas dinner* note. Toss it in the trash.

Grab the grocery list and point the Honda toward the store. Let the car take you to the art museum. Find yourself in front of "Mill at Limetz." Find yourself in front of "Guanyin of the

Southern Sea." Feel content. Find yourself confused trying to exit the parking lot.

Navigate through stacked-up traffic on your way to the store. Feel the drivers lean forward against their steering wheels at the red lights. Only two shopping days left! Everything must go! Sleigh bells ring, are you listening? You're not part of it; you're an alien floating in an alternate space-time continuum.

Park, and float across the lot.

Pretend you don't see the Salvation Army bell ringer.

Notice the turkeys and hams and tubs of whipped cream in the other carts.

Toss your bag of frozen dinners into your back seat.

Loneliness encases you like a casket. The casket walls press against your arms and the top of your head. Feel the coffin lowered into the ground, shovels of heavy dirt raining down on the lid. You can't see. You can't breathe. You don't want to.

After a block, that whole feeling evaporates. Your car is in drive, but your body and mind are in neutral.

Pull into your driveway and discover you left the living room light on for the plants, and now the interior is backlit through the etched glass of the front door. Notice the sight of it feels like opening a present to find exactly what you wanted.

Every few days, your phone rings. Expect it to be Ben, even though there's no cell phone service where he is. Think this is what it will feel like if he dies before you do.

Lie in bed, read, feel drowsiness coming on. Nothing happened today. No museum. No grocery store. No today. There is only the bedroom. Right before sleep descends, understand there's no bedroom.

December 24.

Fold clothes that are bunched up at the foot of the bed. Vacuum.

Sweep away a cobweb from the ceiling near the window. Dust the nightstands and the headboard with lemon oil. Take a whiff. So clean.

For dinner, treat yourself to pizza and a fire in the fireplace. Pop a movie into the DVD player. After the credits roll, you don't want to go upstairs to bed. The flames flicker and wrap a smoky scent around you. You want to linger. Stretch out on the couch with a book. Let your fingertip relish the soft edges of the pages. Ask, "What are you doing?" Sleep there, in front of the fire.

December 25.

Bundle up for your morning walk. It's only fifteen degrees. Even though there's no snow (curse the weatherman for making you worry for nothing), marvel at the stark beauty of winter. Naked branches of oak and cypress trees, evergreens poking into a steely gray sky. The shocking quiet in the middle of the city. Feel the urge to tiptoe.

You stop abruptly further down the block. Someone has parked too many cars in their driveway. Your tidy neighborhood usually has nothing out of place. Two-car garages. Two cars per house. Weave a C-shaped path around the cars, into the street, and back onto the sidewalk.

Wait. Turn around. One, two, three—six cars. What's going on? Football party so early in the morning?

Family visiting … from out of town.

Realize: Today is … Christmas.

Wonder when it happened. Was it Christmas before the overflowing driveway, back there under the steely gray sky, beneath the naked oaks? Did Christmas arrive in one of those six cars?

Picture the travelers crowded into the house, children in sleeping bags on the floor near the tree. Are they awake yet? Are the parents saying *wait 'til after breakfast, honey*?

Realize Christmas arrived when you painted that picture.

Feel calm.

Remember when your grown siblings came home to your parents' house for Christmas.

Try to hear the word *honey*. Hear your father ridicule your brother because the handcrafted rug he designed for your sister is taking too long to finish. "You planning to give it to her next year?" Hear your mother count the presents she's bought for each member of the family, because "*somebody* complained about getting fewer than everybody else." Hear the handcuffs snap around your cousin's wrists, the cops helping your father teach her a lesson for hot-wiring your car, even though you didn't press charges and your mother's crying, "Bill, don't do this."

Realize the Christmas you miss never existed.

See your grandmother fighting the front door.

"Where you going?"

"Home."

"You *are* home."

Walk back to your house on this ordinary day.

Wash clothes. Write. Play a Bob Marley CD. Sing off-key. At bedtime, watch a funny movie.

When it ends, sob.

You speculate you killed Christmas, and you're grieving its loss. Then speculate you're grieving the loss of a past you never had. Sense that it doesn't matter.

Blow your nose.

Picture Ben on retreat, meditating with the other retreatants under the gaze of a golden Buddha statue. Say, "Night, Sweetheart. I miss you."

Catch a faint scent of lemon oil. Take a whiff. So clean.

APPLE PIE FOR TWO

I wiped the butter off the laptop and then reveled in the aroma of cinnamon that filled my astonished kitchen.

Hubby burst through the door. "Something smells delicious in here."

Grinning, I could hardly get the words out. "Baked you a present, honey."

An apple pie cooled on the counter, in direct rebuttal to the fact I hated cooking and wasn't even that crazy about eating.

Ben clapped his hand to his chest. "Wowser, sweetheart. It's beautiful."

It was.

A golden volcano with juice seeping through its fissures and steam escaping its peak. The dish exceeded my culinary skills. I'd attempted it partly because Ben had mentioned he loved homemade apple pie, but mostly because he didn't expect it. He had cheered every uninspired meal I'd set in front of him. His patience had engendered both my gratitude and bravery.

"You did this for me?" he asked.

The question hung in the air. I savored it.

There was nothing to savor about the food I'd grown up with. My father caught catfish in the days when sophisticated palates scorned it as a bottom feeder. He hunted squirrel, coon, duck, and beaver, accompanied by hounds that were breadwinners, rather than pets. Mama baked the coon with barbecue sauce—a failed attempt to disguise its bitter taste. Potatoes and carrots swam around it in a puddle of grease.

In the summer, she picked dandelion greens out of our yard and rutabagas that grew back by the alley. As I picked alongside her, Des Moines' hard-packed clay soil dug into my knees, while mosquitoes tormented a spot above my elbow. I knelt for hours; it seemed a mountain of raw greens cooked down to only a slimy spoonful. Sometimes corn-on-the-cob appeared in our kitchen, sacks full of it. Sweet corn tasted like a reward, but shucking it was punishment, especially for me, squeamish about the worms that lurked beneath the silk.

About once a year, Mama baked fudge. Blocks heavy as bricks sat in the icebox wrapped in waxed paper. She doled out tiny chunks to us kids. It was hard and cold against my front teeth when I bit into a slice. With six in the family, every one nursing a voracious sweet tooth, the fudge disappeared after a day or two. Dad claimed the bulk of it.

When Mama fixed another of Dad's favored treats, he didn't have to share. Nobody else liked chitlins—pig intestines, which she washed in the kitchen sink, then boiled all day long. Their stench dug claws into my throat and lungs. The house stunk for weeks.

Toiling over stove and sink, Mama was borne around the kitchen on a tide of hardscrabble routine, which crowded out any notion of teaching her little girl how to cook. I perched on a step stool in the corner, absent any desire to learn. In those days, *want*—whether the object was Mama's attention, a new doll, or an extra piece of fudge—got you nowhere.

Dad and Mama divorced the year I turned twelve. He married Kim Carol, who preferred poetry and metaphysics to the culinary arts. Concerned about my lethargy, she took me to a doctor, who diagnosed low blood sugar. The doctor explained my new relationship with food—eat every three hours every day—as though he were prescribing antibiotics. Mother Kim found no joy in cooking and didn't help search for recipes that would benefit my health. By the time she entered my life, I had already absorbed subliminal messages from Mama that only the wife fixed the family meals. When Mother Kim relegated me to salad making, my kitchen education stagnated at rinsing lettuce and washing dishes.

Meanwhile, she struggled to maintain the Elizabeth Taylor figure of her twenties. Sweets were banned. Tab replaced Kool-Aid. When I was in college, she warned if my thighs developed saddlebags, I'd never get rid of them, and so cajoled me to join her in fad diets. Her mantra: "We'll lose five pounds this weekend."

During the years spent with Mama, meal preparation was synonymous with forced labor. Mother Kim did nothing to dissuade me of that view, and in fact, after she came into my life, food became a bitter pill.

I found the apple pie recipe online at a blog called *Food Wishes: Video Recipes with Chef John*. His initial instruction, "peel and core the apples," tightened my mouth into a grimace. The words fell through a hole in my chest, a space where other women stored cooking lessons learned from mom.

Surely Chef John would glare out from the computer screen, the way Mother Kim had during my first visit home as a married woman. When I'd hesitated at the stove, her impatience had wilted me: "You can't even make gravy? How in the world do you feed your husband?"

Here's how. I laid out *The Joy of Cooking*, a dictionary, and three tablets on my kitchen table. I flipped the cookbook open to the beef chapter, read through a recipe until an unfamiliar word, like *braise*, popped up. Looked up *braise* in the dictionary. If it sounded do-able, I returned to the recipe, copied all the ingredients, including measurements, onto a grocery list—tablet number one. When the recipe required an unusual utensil, like a roasting pan, I listed that on tablet number two (after looking it up in the dictionary). Next, a perusal of the chicken chapter, followed by fish, casseroles, and vegetables. On tablet number three, the days of the week. Beside each day, a menu. At the grocery store, I studied labels to determine which size of block cheese would produce half a cup shredded. Gadgets required a stop at Target on the way home. And what distinguished a spatula from a pancake turner? I repeated the process every week, because my cupboards held none of the essentials. Staples? They fastened papers together.

I pushed play on Chef John's video. The camera focused on his hands, a knife in one, an apple in the other. He cut off the ends, and then peeled around. "I don't have any tricks for that. Just use a paring knife. You can use a peeler." He cut the fruit in quarters and then sliced off the cores. "I'm not a big corer. I don't have one of those things you push through. Actually I think I do have one, but it's rusty."

What did he say? I pushed rewind. "… use a paring knife … " and then "…one of those things you push through." Chef John dismissed gadgets as optional. I wanted to kiss him.

I studied the comments below the typed recipe. Question: Won't the bottom crust be soggy? Chef responded, "I've never really thought about it." Question: Forgot to dot the apples with butter. Will it be okay? Chef responded, "Should be okay." Question: What about store-bought crusts? Response, "Just fine." How do you get the first piece of pie out? "It might fall apart. That's normal."

I practically memorized the recipe, comments, and video—determined to root out deception. Desperate to identify any turn of a phrase that, misunderstood, would lead to humiliation. My faith grew. Let Chef John hold my hand; I would end up with pie.

"Bye, honey. See you tonight." After Ben left the house for the day, I set up my laptop on the kitchen counter. The tinkle of Oscar Peterson's mellow jazz piano floated from our CD player. Apple peel ribbons dropped into the sink. Knife clacked against cutting board. "Ow." I knocked my forehead against an open cabinet door, rubbed the sore spot with a sticky hand. That's okay, keep going. The counter turned white from spilled cornstarch and sugar. I stirred—*damn, is it too wet?* Rewound the video. "… going to be really juicy," Chef John said. An errant peel squished underfoot. I poured the goopy mixture into a crust-lined pie plate, popping a slice into my mouth. Crunchy and sweet. For heaven's sake—delicious. But too many apples, the top crust will never fit. Checked the video again. My concoction matched the freeze frame of Chef John's unbaked pie. The top crust broke when I eased it on. No problem. Pinch it together. I painted the whole thing with beaten egg, in careless swipes just like Chef. Hot air hit my face when I opened the oven door to slide the pie inside.

I had just Windexed the laptop screen and was blowing sugar from the keyboard when our motorized garage door announced Ben's arrival.

He burst into the kitchen. "Something smells delicious in here."

Snapping the computer shut, I pointed to the pie. "Made you a present, honey."

"Wowser, sweetheart. It's beautiful. Apple?" His forward momentum halted, but his gaze remained fixed on the treat, as though I might snatch it away if he blinked. "You did this for me?"

The first piece out of the pan fell apart. That was normal.

I presented him a saucer heaped with apples, juice, and crust. After scooping up a forkful he closed his eyes to emphasize the *mmmm*.

"Yes, for you," I said. "For both of us."

ON THE PATH

The Ozark Mountains sweep through Oklahoma, Arkansas, and Missouri. Eons have flattened crags and peaks into a plateau of light-blocking forest that squeezes in around local roads. Twenty miles south of Ava, Missouri, a two-lane road narrows to a gravel drive, and after a quarter mile, the trees part and the sun spotlights a clearing. A stake is planted in the gravel. Painted on it, the word *Path*—underscored with an arrow—indicates a trailhead.

Out for a hike on a Friday morning, I paused beside the trailhead sign, mustered all my strength, and kicked the stake. Although pain shot from foot to knee, I didn't mind. The impact rewarded me with a resounding thwack that broke nature's silence. Silence could kill you. Silence was the dead air of your bedroom when nightmares froze screams too deep in your throat to bring Mama running. Where were you? In a coffin? In bed? In a swamp?

You're awake Dawn, out for a hike in the woods.

Stations of the Cross were posted along the way, a Catholic practice that meant nothing to me, but might provide diversion from my mind's habitual predictions of disaster. The first Station—a hand-made cross shoulder high and fashioned from oak limbs—rose from the underbrush, growing there as naturally as the oaks that surrounded it. A wooden sign was attached to the top. Painted black and tacked to a board, individually hand-carved letters read *Judged*. It could have been someone's idea of a practical joke, had anyone else been around. Self-judgment was a reflex, indistinguishable from my pulse.

In my fifties, I began attending meditation retreats, the retreat centers invariably located in remote wooded areas. During evening sessions, seekers whispered their gratitude for escape from the city, declared how peaceful it was in the woods. They reported experiences of oneness while camping. The teacher hinted yes … maybe … time spent in the natural world might lead to the timelessness of truth. But I'd seen a documentary about a man who'd felt a kinship with grizzlies and had holed up in a cabin to film winter in their midst. Footage was found inside his camera. The final frames were jerky shots of floor, and chair legs, and kicking feet. Screams. Then silence.

As sunlight filtered through the Ozark canopy, I was afraid of the pierce of canine teeth and afraid foul spittle would drip onto my face and afraid the dying would be slow … painful … lonely.

I was bone tired of being afraid.

The well-trodden path—wide and flat—presented no physical challenge. Pines offered up the scent of Christmas trees, which said there was nothing to worry about.

A scrabble in the underbrush said grizzly.

Thickening vegetation loomed on either side. Tendrils twined around tree trunks and crept across the leafy ceiling, shrouding the passageway in gloom. The woods were closing in.

Another cross.

Carries.

I was a mule carrying a trunk-load of terrified, crumpling under the weight.

A faint gurgle sounded in the distance. Odors of bark and loam gave way, and the air smelled like rain had just passed through. The path bottomed out at a creek, a sight that brought a sigh of relief, because the trail featured eight creek crossings, and here was the first. I stepped onto a flat rock midstream and jumped across, which put me at the foot of a bank. A bench sat at the top of the bank, a goal that promised a resting spot and maybe a good view, too.

In spite of those promises, and in spite of the sun warming my face, I shivered. My skin crawled. The effort to keep going was like pushing against the wind. That was no resting spot up there; it was a dead-end. Shadows were assailants that raked claws against my back.

Those are trees, not assailants. Limbs, not claws. Don't let the shadows win. What's that … under the bench?

I spun toward home, nearly crashing into another cross.

Gamble.

The commandment slammed into my chest.

Take a risk. For once.

I risked another step toward the bench. But only one.

I raced back to the trailhead, and reaching it, bent over panting, hands on knees, my chest a bellows.

Coward. Always giving up.

Atop a small rise stood another cross. The sign, with its hand-lettered message, was dangling by a single nail.

Compassion.

I traced the letters with a fingertip. Carved shapes worn smooth, the curves of *m* and *s* slowing my mind's race toward condemnation.

On Saturday morning the woods seemed less likely to be harboring grizzlies or psychopaths. Squirrels barked and my boots crunched lightly through fallen leaves. From *Judged,* I waded across the stream and climbed to *Gamble,* stopping beside the bench. Instead of a scenic overlook, the seat faced a blind curve. No point in lingering. Just around the bend—a cross, so unexpected I almost ran into it.

Crucified.

I doubled over, sucker-punched. The same sucker punch as decades earlier—the phone call about Dad. His final hours in the hospital. Gone? It couldn't be possible. We were going to breakfast at his favorite diner. We were going to hang out on his patio, talking politics. He'd befriended the entire population of my hometown; it was time for him to be my friend. Faced straight on, the Dad-shaped emptiness would have crushed me.

I turned away from *Crucified.*

The word disappeared from view; my pace picked up from stumble to stride; and its rhythm brought the singsong of ordinary. Right, left. Tromp, tromp. One foot, the other. Until, that is, my legs and arms began to tremble. The undergrowth rustled. A beast that bided its time. Scudding clouds alternately threw the path into darkness, then stabbed it with sunlight. Raised hairs on the back of my neck demanded I turn back. Now. Right now.

Another cross.

Died.

It sucked the air from my lungs. The blood from my cheeks. The ground from beneath my feet.

I was suspended like an executed man, the trap door sprung.

Died?

Obliterated.

I heard a scratch in a pile of fallen leaves, and the scratch could hear me as well. Pine needles could smell the lavender lotion on my skin. As I reached out, the air parted around my hand. Rocks gave under my weight. Evergreens reached, stretched, extended skyward, animated by the very intention that straightens my spine in mountain pose. A pale crescent moon hung above the horizon, and I looked back at myself from the lunar surface. I could never be lost. I was everywhere.

Rational thought wrestled for control. Too soon, the thinking mind reclaimed authority, snatching me away from dimensions more dangerous than grizzlies. Safety lay within clearly defined boundaries: streets that shaped neighborhoods, fences that carved yards, walls that boxed in the familiar.

Everywhere was too big.

On Sunday, I was drawn to the trail like a driver slowing to peer at an accident.

I was the accident.

I'd tucked a pen and pad into my pocket.

The plan: Hike as far as the second creek crossing; declare victory; turn back. Once again, it was an easy stroll downhill to the valley where the creek washed over the path. Two strides to the other side. I sidestepped around a cross I hadn't noticed before, no hand-lettered sign attached to its transverse bar. My foot brushed a flat square object half buried in mud.

Wome-

Women. Missing the *n*. What women? Wives, lovers, aunties, or sisters, time had reduced them to a lowly state. What was their story? Invisible and forgotten? Imaginary? I knelt in the leaves, brushed debris from the weathered wood, and cradled it in my palms, as a mother might touch the cheek of a child disturbed by a dream. A female presence hovered near the earth, a stillness that gave birth to the sounds high above: call of an owl, tap of a woodpecker. Close to the ground, there was a softening around my own story, loneliness fading.

A search for errant nails proved futile, so I propped the sign against the foot of the cross, leaving *Women* to keep vigil for the lonely and the lost.

The land sloped uphill to *Gamble*. The bench was tempting, a perch from which to mark one's bearings, to contemplate one's journey, but I moved on, pausing at *Crucified* and then again at *Died*. The spells they'd cast on Saturday no longer captivated.

The trail switch-backed into dense scrub that made me check over my shoulder. Only a few feet of the path was visible; then it disappeared around a turn. Did the ground fall away? Was it pitched too steep? Did it plummet off a cliff?

Another cross.

Descent.

I scuffed downhill, and at the bottom, a bridge fashioned from branches spanned the stream. The second crossing.

I made it.

My whoops rang through the valley. "Oh yeah. Did it, did it, did it." A triumphant dance skipped me to the center of the bridge. "Did it, did it, did it." I flung my pencil into the air and caught it one-handed. "Did it, did it, did it." I took victory laps back and forth across the span. Hopped onto dry land. Struck a pose, hands on hips. Confidence was a new feeling.

There were more woods to explore—and no reason to turn back. For the first time all weekend, I wanted to hike the trail simply because I could.

The brook meandered alongside and over the footpath, the path as much *in* the creek as it was *crossing* the creek. I forded three times in quick succession, before the trail widened into a sandbar.

With the bridge out of view, there was no indication a human had ever passed this way. It brought me to a standstill. Up until that moment, on the lookout for threats, always on edge about getting lost, I had trudged along wide-eyed but had never seen the view. Nature was brazenly gorgeous.

A trail sandwiched between bluff and stream, a wooded bank

on the other side of the stream. The valley was thrown into relief, as if I were wearing 3D glasses. Oak branches thrust themselves toward me (I felt the urge to duck) and invaded the personal space of neighboring cedars. Pines shot their barbed spears up through the spreading oaks, while exposed roots snaked downward along the face of the bluff until they disappeared into the stream—a stream whose bed lay fathoms beneath the surface, inducing vertigo when I looked.

I was eager to lose myself in the brazen beauty of other valleys. Wait.

Hadn't I been standing on a wide flat trail? On dry land? Looking back toward the spot where the bridge should have been … all I could see was creek.

The path was gone.

I couldn't breathe. Then breathed too fast, sucked into childhood nightmares once again, clawing my way to awake. Where was I?

A wisp of a suggestion floated toward my consciousness: *Dawn, the creek is the path.* But the suggestion petered out, swallowed by the roar of blood rushing into my temples. Shaking, about to lose my balance, I wobbled backward onto a rock. The stone poked the bottom of my foot. *Follow the creek.*

My mind raced. *It's panic time, girl. You're lost.*

My feet stood firm. *The creek is the path.*

Solid creek bed lay under the bubbling surface. I was on the ground, as well as in the water. A refrain from Saturday came to mind, like a blessing: *I could never be lost. I was everywhere.*

I needed steady balance before venturing forward on slippery rocks. I pulled the notepad from my pocket. *Lost. Creek. Path.* No more than timid hen scratches, the letters resembled an old woman's gnarled fingers, but the scrape of pen across paper calmed me. I inched ahead, arms spread. My center of gravity shifted.

There was the bluff on my right, the slope on my left, the bridge ahead.

At my feet, intermittent dry spots pointed out the now-obvious trail, connecting the dots to the bridge. I stepped onto the reassuring man-made surface, a structure whose craftsmanship had previously escaped my notice. Branches were meticulously braided together. Constant moisture in the air had colored the wood a rich brown, the mahogany interrupted by lighter streaks, where the craftsman had scraped away knots, exposing pale flesh. Off to the right stood the sages, *Crucified* and *Died*. We exchanged a *namasté*.

I crested the hill and was welcomed by *Descent*. The bench was waiting around the bend. While I rested there, *Gamble* kept me company. Continuing, I retraced my steps downhill to the creek crossing that lay nearest the trailhead. I bounded across in a single leap. The trail broadened. I knew it would. As I knew the canopy would close around a shady spot, and then the route would wind uphill to a clearing. The path had nothing more to teach me.

But in that cocky instant, my feet planted on terra firma, having finally found purchase on earth and in my psyche—my knees buckled.

I sank onto the hard-packed dirt, a peasant forced to kneel before a king, and hesitated—shocked and humbled—before raising my gaze.

A cross was tucked into a nook, protected from the elements. Neither wind nor rain had penetrated the treetops to fade the letters, arranged into words that were legible even in dim light.

Falls Down.

"Yes," I said, then got up and let the path lead me home.

SHOWING UP

Geoffrey adjusted the shoulder strap on his ball gown. "I promised I'd wear this."

The mourners who filled the church erupted in appreciative laughter. Pastel pink was not my color (although I could have pulled off the sequins). On me, the tiara would have been too much. And *I* would have tripped over the stilettos Geoffrey was wearing. So I clasped my hands together in deep admiration at his graceful entrance amid his voluminous chiffon skirt.

An hour earlier, my friend's memorial service had begun solemnly. A gentleman in a dark suit, head down, trudged across the stage to the lectern. His face was shadowed in loss, his steps perhaps reticent to take on the day's responsibility. Although his name has been buried under other images from the day, he looked like a Geoffrey to me. After adjusting the microphone, he waved his arms to indicate the packed sanctuary. "We all loved Bob and he loved us."

The crowd murmured in assent.

I raised an eyebrow. Bob had been a first-rate charmer with a lightning wit and a full-body laugh, but I doubted every mourner in attendance had known him well enough to claim love. Besides, I suspected nefarious motives of anyone who'd collected enough friends to fill a medium-sized church.

Geoffrey continued. "Bob kept friends separated into different silos, possibly so he could tell a story seventeen times without anybody knowing he was repeating it. Today we recognize the different aspects of his life. So please stand when I name the place where you knew him. Grade school—."

Surely I'd heard that wrong. Grade school? How was it possible a man in his sixties could be paid tribute by his grade school chums? The only person I remembered from grade school was Tommy Jones. He'd proclaimed his love for me right there in the cafeteria, just before inviting me to look under the table, where his one-eyed monster was squirming around outside his pants. I certainly hoped Tommy would refrain from attending my funeral. Would any other grade school chums remember me? What had I achieved back then that a former classmate might recall half a century later, while perusing the obituary section? "Oh, honey, what a shame. Dawn Downey passed away. Always admired her form on the jungle gym."

Bob must have been a stand-out on the jungle gym, because sixty of his grammar school chums rose to their feet.

Geoffrey said, "College friends."

Now there was an oxymoron. As an undergrad, I'd suffered from severe awkwardness, which I'd treated with pot. I overcame both and by graduation, Yolanda—another senior—and I were hanging out in each other's dorm rooms, claiming to be studying, but actually discussing comparative male anatomy. Had my college offered Friendship 101, I would have flunked it. I didn't realize Yolanda was my best friend until ten years into our relationship. She'll earn sainthood for her loyalty, since well into middle age I remained clueless about the importance of telephones and email. When the reaper collects me, I hope to goodness somebody lets her know. Otherwise she'll assume I've just forgotten to call.

Apparently Bob never forgot to call. Seven hundred pals from his alma mater stood.

"Social Security."

His former co-workers. They were on their feet and hooting. It surprised me to learn Bob had been a cog in the federal bureaucracy. It also surprised me that government workers hooted. I couldn't deny their obvious affection for the deceased. Still, demonstrativeness aside, mixing love and government was just asking for trouble.

"Gay, lesbian, bisexual, transgendered."

Another couple thousand rose, resembling the cast of "La Cage aux Folles." I scowled at the thought of my own gay friends, consistently bland in their t-shirts and accountant haircuts. Why couldn't they wear colors and look more like Bob's buddies? And why didn't I have any transgendered friends? (Hmm, maybe I did.)

Geoffrey droned on through the list of Bob Subcultures. Family. Foodies: food servers, fast-food cashiers, dining companions. Hospice folks: patients, staff, fellow volunteers. Neighbors. This category impressed me, because if your neighbors liked you, it meant you were on your best behavior even when you thought nobody was looking.

"Did I leave anybody out?"

A white-haired woman waved her hand. It took a while for Geoffrey to spot her among the 80,000 people who were on their feet.

She said, "Writers."

"Oh, yes. I forgot. He was also writing for the last few years."

Did he say *also* writing? Bob had participated in two weekly writing groups, on-line writing communities; writers retreats and conferences. He'd taught workshops and edited a magazine. Because of these activities, not to mention his essays, novels, short stories, and poetry, I'd assumed Bob was a writer. *Also writing* implied he'd accomplished these things while maintaining an active social life with non-writers. That was just showing off.

After the masses reclaimed their seats, a woman replaced Geoffrey behind the lectern. She read a letter from Natalie Goldberg, an author whose name was hallowed among writers and Buddhists. (As a current writer and former Buddhist, I can assure you gaining fame within these two constituencies is a huge achievement, since both groups spend all of their time not talking.) Bob had studied with Ms. Goldberg for a decade and had attended her annual writers' retreat frequently enough to call her Natalie. She'd sent a letter of condolence to those of us gathered at his memorial service. Natalie Goldberg was sorry for our loss.

That should have been my letter. Never mind she didn't know I existed. Never mind I hadn't attended her retreat. Never mind I'd read only one (almost the whole thing) of her books. Never mind I'd long since stopped calling myself a Buddhist. Natalie Goldberg didn't know that. If she were half as smart as we who worshiped her assumed, she'd intuit the depth of my talent (I was probably the next Natalie Goldberg) and therefore write a letter offering condolences for the loss of me. (Never mind I was still alive.)

When Geoffrey reappeared enveloped in pink chiffon, my jealousy evaporated.

"I promised Bob I'd wear this," he said, followed by something I could not hear over the applause that accompanied his entrance.

Mourners began shuffling toward the stage, until only two of us were left in our seats.

"What's going on?" I asked the other guy.

"Testimonials," he replied.

The procession lasted over a week.

"Bob remembered my mother's cousin's birthday."

"He brought me flowers after my hamster died."

I felt a lump in my throat.

"He visited my dad in the hospital."

My shoulders slumped.

"He helped me plant petunias."

Each story was met with nods and sniffles.

I nodded, too, my own memory jogged. Citing our friendship, Bob had once objected when another writer had sprinkled the *N* word throughout his prose—and I hadn't even been in the room. I had witnessed neither the offense nor Bob's defense of my feelings. Later I found out he'd said, "What if Dawn were here?"

I should have worn a ball gown in his honor.

A Taco Bell cashier, still in uniform, made her way to the microphone. Her voice trembled. "Afraid I'd be late. I just got off work." She raised a tissue to her nose. "Bob came in maybe twice a month. Sometimes with another guy. He always talked to me. A few days ago, his friend came in alone. I said, 'Where's my buddy' … and then … he told me." She cleared her throat.

I calculated the logistics leading up to her presence in the church, that her time within Bob's orbit had engendered emotions worthy of such logistics—that still dressed in her uniform, she'd ridden the bus across town for the chance to say goodbye.

Showing up. It was an act you could not fake. Maybe love was as simple as that.

Thanks, Bob.

ACKNOWLEDGMENTS

The author gratefully acknowledges the following publications where essays first appeared, sometimes in different form.

Kansas City Voices: "Tango for Frankie"
Persimmon Tree: "The Cleaning Women"
Punctuate: "How to Survive Christmas Alone"
River, Blood, and Corn: "A Traveler's Tale," previously titled "Postcards"
Skirt! Magazine: "Good Bones"
The Christian Science Monitor: "Bah Humbug"

"Impermanence" also appeared in *Stumbling toward the Buddha: Stories about Tripping over My Principles on the Road to Transformation*

"How to Survive Christmas Alone" also appeared in *River, Blood, and Corn*

A big thank you goes out to:

WTF critique group—Jessica Conoley, Karin Frank, Annie Raab, Teresa Vratil, and Dane Zeller—for having high standards and coaxing cohesive stories from my typewritten pages.

Teresa Mandala, cover designer, for once again translating my emotions into a spot-on image. And for our ongoing, ever-expanding collaboration in art and friendship.

Marcia Meier, developmental editor. Marcia tells me when a manuscript has finally turned into a book.

Julie Tenenbaum, copy editor, for keeping my stories spotless in the grammar-spelling-typo department. And for always looking forward to my next book.

Randy Leclair for the Palomino art pencils ("half the pressure, twice the speed"), which I use to get inspiration flowing.

Katherine Guendling for her insights about "The Cleaning Women" and "On the Path."

Michelle Downey Lawyer for telling me to write with confidence.

Michael Downey for calling me *brilliant*.

Stephanie Carey, Jim Cosgrove, Victor Dougherty, Eric Durham, Kate Miller, Roxanne Sloate, and Mark Theis, who shared their silent retreat with me. Their collective meditation energy resulted in "How to Survive Christmas Alone."

All the subscribers to my blog for their steady encouragement and heartfelt emails. And for expecting to see me in their inboxes every Friday. They keep me writing.

My yoga teachers—Nancy Bounds and Carolyn Celestine—for teaching me to pay attention to the details and breathe, which are essential skills for writing.

Kelli Austin for showing me how to be brave outside ... in nature ... where ticks and spiders hide, so I can go to the scary places in writing.

Ben Worth, my husband, for always getting my jokes, which is the truest expression of love.

ABOUT THE AUTHOR

Dawn Downey is the author of *From Dawn to Daylight: Essays*, a collection of personal vignettes. She is also the author of a memoir, *Stumbling toward the Buddha: Stories about Tripping over My Principles on the Road to Transformation*.

Publications featuring her essays include *Kansas City Voices*; *Persimmon Tree*; *Punctuate*; *River, Blood, and Corn*; *Shambhala Sun*, and *Skirt! Magazine*.

She writes to bring people together in a compassionate understanding of one another. By composing essays about her personal challenges, she learns the workings of her mind. When her followers respond by sharing anecdotes from their own lives, she learns that most minds work in a similar fashion. She is driven to share her stories by the hope that readers will lovingly accept those similarities—in themselves, in fellow travelers, and in their adversaries.

Downey lives in Kansas City, Missouri, with her husband, Ben Worth.

If you enjoyed *Searching for My Heart*, sign up for her blog at DawnDowney.com.